Living in Gods Rest

How we live an abundant life

© Copyright Lynda Wade 2014

Living in God's Rest

"Most assuredly I say to you, he who does not enter the sheepfold by the door, but climbs up some other way, the same is a thief and a robber. But he who enters by the door is the shepherd of the sheep. To him the doorkeeper opens and the sheep hear his voice and he calls his own sheep by name and leads them out. And when he brings out his own sheep he goes before them and the sheep follow him for they know his voice. Yet they will by no means follow a stranger, but will flee from him for they do not know the voice of strangers...........Most assuredly I say to you I am the door of the sheep. All who ever came before Me are thieves and robbers, but the sheep did not hear them. I am the door. If anyone enters by me he will be saved and will go in and out and find pasture. The thief does not come except to steal and to kill and to destroy. I have come that they may have life and that they may have it more abundantly"[1]

In the Middle East the flocks of sheep are all herded together into one pen for the night through a single gate. Each shepherd takes his turn to be the watchman over them, guarding against attack by wild animals. In the morning each shepherd comes to the gate and calls to his sheep and they all come to him and follow him leaving the other sheep behind, because they know the sound of his voice.

Jesus says that He is the gate; the way in to safety and care. Through him we find pasture and a place to be. He warns us that although we may be sheep who know him and have even gone through the gate to safety it doesn't exempt us from that which would steal us away. He tells us that it will not blatantly approach the gate but will creep in through the back door.

The thief of time, peace, integrity, and belief will always choose to disguise itself in need, choice, and self sufficiency world view. Jesus warns that the thief has come to ultimately destroy all of those things; to take our time with meaningless pursuits, give extra work to fill our purses to buy more and keep us from our family. We will be deceived into believing it is our responsibility to work harder, to earn more to live normally as everyone else does, instead of understanding it is God who says 'I will provide'. We will choose to do this and it can ultimately destroy the peace in our hearts and, for some, our families and our homes.

Peace is the rest we have when we enter the sheep pen through Jesus. It is the first flush of faith that is pure and strong and it is a target for our enemy to chip away at until it gets to the point where we have to fight to get it back. The world says that we are mad to live by faith, to stand believing and trusting in a God who loves us and wants nothing for us but joy, peace, care and love, who looks to provide us with health and comfortable living. Who says He will, and then backs it with action. We are told that we should be self sufficient, self taught and self disciplined, beholden to no-one, not even to God, and that we should strive to excel. Even within the church family we take that responsibility to heart and spend much time working for God, less time listening to Him, more time thinking we know the way and less time waiting for Him to tell us.

What kind of believer do we want to be? Do you feel you are on a hamster wheel of working, both inside and outside the church? Do you long to just be led, not to worry, and to have complete peace and confidence in God's ability to get you there?

Living in Gods rest is not a remit to do nothing Paul tells us that we are 'living out' our faith here on earth. However it is how and why we do things that is important, not what we do. Are we happy for God to be in charge? Or are we on a pathway of listening to ourselves?

Take the time at the end of each session to sit quietly with God and discern what He is saying to you. May God bless you and the family you represent as you read this book.

Lynda Wade

Chapter 1

What is Rest?

As He was preparing the disciples to see Him go back to His Father in heaven, Jesus turned to them and said in John 14 v 12;

"Most assuredly, I say to you, he who believes in me, the works that I do he will do also: and greater works than these he will do because I go to my Father".

That is a massive statement that Jesus is making, and one which few of us rise to. The question that comes to mind is this: Why then is it that after giving us all that He has, we as a people struggle to live the life He promised?

For most of us the ideal is to be the Christian we read about seemingly everywhere; strong, full of faith, quick to repent and forgive, non judgemental and full of love, exhibiting all of the spiritual gifts and involved in church. The reality is that while these things are not wrong to want, for many of us, we struggle to meet them as a daily act in our lives. Life gets in the way, time seems to evaporate and we end up running around like headless chickens. The result is that we end up disheartened, defeated and working hard to prove to those around us that we really are maturing in the Lord because that is what we think we should be doing.

However God's perspective is far different. From the beginning the Father- heart of God has longed to do five things:

- To be in relationship with mankind
- To set us free from the control of sin
- To empower and equip us
- To provide for and lead us into the entirety of what He offers.
- To have a people who worship Him; giving worth to Him through their thoughts and actions

You will notice that all of these points come from God and not us. It was His idea to have a relationship with His creation, His idea to provide a way back from the fall and set us free from the control of sin, His idea to empower us and equip us, and His idea to provide for and lead us. All so we can bring our worship to Him and put Him in His proper place in our lives

Paul writes in Romans 8 v31 *"What, then, shall we say in response to these things? If God is for us, who can be against us?"* God has, through Jesus, made us conquerors, joint inheritors of a kingdom, with the ability to walk on this earth redeemed, and sanctified by His death and resurrection. That is our position, the place we are in right at this moment. It is the truth behind our faith. You may not feel that but I will say this, feelings are transitory and dependant on a whole host of factors, truth is truth. And the truth is that through salvation all of the above is fact and no matter how many times we deny it or allow the enemy to steal it from us it will still stand.

In Hebrews 4 v 1-5 the writer says this;

"Therefore, since a promise remains of entering into His rest, let us fear lest any of you come short of it. For indeed the gospel was preached to us as well as to them; but the word which they heard did not profit them, not being mixed with faith in those who heard it..."

And in Hebrews 4 v 9-10 *"There remains therefore a rest for the people of God. For he who has entered His rest has himself also ceased from His works as God did from His".*

So God first of all promises a rest for His people, those who have taken that step; entered into the sheep pen and become part of the family of God through salvation. God's promise is like no other, it is a legally binding word that stands for eternity and comes from his heart. So what is His rest?

There are two key moments in history that point the way to discovering what it is. The first quoted here in Hebrews *"Thus the heavens and the earth and all the host of them were finished. And on the seventh day God ended His work which He had done and He rested...."*[2]. The second happened several thousand years later on a hill just outside Jerusalem and is recorded in Johns gospel *'So when Jesus had received the sour wine, He *said "It is finished" and bowing His head, He gave up His spirit.₃'* [The meaning here of it being finished is that mans debt to God had been paid]. In both cases God the Father and God the Son rested in the conclusion of their missions. God had completed Creation; Jesus had completed Salvation and brought the work of redemption to absolute closure. And because of these two moments those of us who take up the offer of salvation enter into God's completion. When God offers 'rest' for those who believe, He is offering completion.

Now 'completion' means just that. Nothing more can be done or said that will enhance what God has done, especially nothing that we could do. After all, righteousness is of God and not us. However as much as we know in our heads that Jesus has done it all we still find ourselves thinking sometimes that somehow, if we did things a little better, prayed harder, read more scripture, loved deeper... the list goes on ....that we would be better Christians. However this is simply not the case and the key is in Hebrew 4 verse 10; *"For he who entered His rest has himself also ceased from his works, as God did from His"*

We must understand that if we have entered into His rest through our salvation then it is finished for us. We have come to a place in God where we no longer have to **work** at our relationship with Him or others. He has done it all. From the point of salvation onward, there is nothing we need to or indeed can do. We are who we are, and in partnership with Him by the power of the

Holy Spirit we will be discipled into the people He wants us to be by Him, so that He can equip and use us in the Kingdom of God.

The problem is that we are taught not to do that but to take the responsibility for our faith journey into our own hands. That would be okay if we had an idea of what we needed to do, but man is imperfect and most of the time we really do not have a clue of what we need in order for us to truly grow. And to be fair church can sometimes not exactly help the situation. Discipleship is rarely practiced as it should be. If we look at the model Jesus created as our blueprint the twelve disciples were seldom away from His side. And He operated in a 'you watch me do it, I watch you do it, you do' policy. The teaching He imparted was personal and the relationships He created were deep. We have courses that we run, and although there is usually a second tier of teaching that follows on taking new Christians deeper it won't have that one to one deep teaching that Jesus emulates.

Generally speaking churches seldom have an ongoing program of discipleship that encompasses the whole body and if and when they do it is not sustained past the normal six week point which seems to be the length of anything we do. The churches that operate a small group system headed up with mature believers willing and able to truly help in discipling are the ones that usually do best in this area, and I would encourage you if your church does this to sign up and take part in it.

In the early days of our journey some of the teaching we take on board is unhelpful for us because we are not spiritually mature enough to access it properly. And if we have no one person to go to in order to impart wisdom into what we are learning the result is a people with all manner of differing levels of understanding. Problems arise when we have to struggle alone filtering out good teaching from not so good. The longer we have been a Christian the harder it is for some to say that they don't understand it, let alone try to live it. Learning facts about scripture and the characters and wisdom found within its pages is a doddle compared with applying the truths we learn. And it is the application of the teaching which is vital to success. The result is a lot of trying and a lot of failing and a lot of despondency. Most of us if we are honest even when we are maturing have been to seminars and teaching days over the years to be fired up by what is being taught, then to find that the enthusiasm we had at the conference dwindling because we couldn't seem to live it. Or we've read the latest book that pointed out our shortcomings and we determine to work on them only to fall again after a short time. I've done it myself and I am sure it resonates with some of you reading this right now.

But don't misunderstand me God is not against responsibility, but we have to know what we are responsible for and what is His responsibility. The message of Hebrews 4 is not, "Don't do anything"; it is simply to rest in what God has already done. When we do rest we find ourselves in a place of peace and quiet. Unhurried and tranquil, our soul becomes pliable, not full of discord and apprehension of failure. And that's a place we all need to be in. Spending time with Father God listening and discerning His voice is more precious and of greater value than a thousand seminars or books. Then when you do read or attend meetings you will have the ability to filter out what God wants you to learn from it, instead of desperately taking on teaching which you are unable to process properly at that time.

So if we have accepted God's gift of salvation and we accept that we have already entered into His rest, then why is it still so hard? If you jump into a swimming pool you may be in the water but until you move around you are not swimming. We may be in God's rest as a fact but unless we are living in God's rest we cannot take advantage of the treasure that is waiting for us.

God has provided the place, and in His wisdom He has provided us with the blueprint of how we live in that place. When Jesus came to earth one of the things that He did was to give us a snapshot of what someone living in God's rest looks like. His days, His lifestyle the way He operated gives us a window to look through to see the potential for us.

Before you cry "But He was God" I would beg to slightly differ. And I don't think that's heresy. Jesus gave up all of His royal privilege and position in order to be born a man here on earth. He did it willingly, but if He hadn't He could never identify with us, never experience pain and suffering, never be able to say "I know how you feel". And although He was fully man and fully God with the exception of the forgiveness of sin He never once operated on earth as God. The Jesus we read about in scripture is a man who is living in God's rest, so tuned in to the Father's heart that He only operated in what His Father was telling Him to do. And that is why, when we discover how to live that way too, the reality of the opening statement of chapter one that Jesus makes in John 14 v 12 becomes a possibility.

Time and time again, we see Jesus withdrawing from the crowds and even from His disciples just to spend time with the Father, receiving instructions and being filled with power to replace all that He had given out, resting in their relationship. In Luke chapter 6 v 12 we see Jesus withdrawing to a mountain to pray and He prayed to God all night. At daybreak He called together all of His disciples and chose the twelve to be His inner court, those who would be responsible for carrying the gospel to the nations. This was a vital choice and I dare say on a human level you and I would have chosen differently, however Jesus went straight to Father God and did exactly what He was told to do. Only then did He break the news to the waiting disciples. In John 5 v 30 it says this *"I can of Myself do nothing. As I hear, I judge, and My judgement is righteous because I do not seek My own will but the will of the Father who sent Me"*. If this is how Jesus operated who are we to do differently?

Discovering the entirety of the powerful life that we could and should be living is one of the most valuable lessons that we will ever learn on earth, because it draws us closer to the point of truly becoming more like Jesus, however that fact causes it to be one of the key things that our enemy will try to keep us from discovering, because he knows that when we get hold of this teaching it will transform our walk with God.

Chapter 2

Rest and Responsibility

Hebrews Chapter 6 v 9-12 in the Message says this

'I'm sure that won't happen to you friends. I have better things in mind for you – salvation things! God doesn't miss anything. He knows perfectly well all the love you've shown by helping needy Christians, and that you keep at it. And now I want each of you to extend that same intensity toward a full-bodied hope, and keep at it till the finish. Don't drag your feet. Be like those who stay the course with committed faith and then get everything promised to them'.

In the world most of us who have a hope of getting better at something give up after a while. We stabilise at our own accepted level of competence and content ourselves with staying there. Others continue with a punishing regimen to allow themselves to reach the peak of perfection in their field. Some get to the point where learning or practising becomes too hard or time consuming and stop. The writer to the Hebrews is urging them not to give up but to keep going in faith 'to the finish'. He acknowledges their works but points them on the road of spiritual things when talking about them not giving in. As Christians we are sometimes better at 'keeping going' on the whole 'works' thing than on the spiritual. Helping out at the soup kitchens is sometimes easier that spending those hours alone with God. Here the writer acknowledges both. James says "*For as the body without the spirit is dead so faith without works is dead also*"[4] You see which way round it is, if our spiritual life is on track then out of that flows the action to back it, not the other way round. If we treat our spiritual journey as we treat other things, sitting back and being content with an acceptable level of understanding, we will not only be unfulfilled we will also be doing God a disservice.

God doesn't want us to strive, but He does want us to grow. So how do we do that? How does the 'rest' fit in with being diligent and disciplined and thinking about what we do and achieve in and for the Kingdom of God?

It's all about the toothbrush!

Every day we get up, go to the bathroom, shower or wash and clean our teeth, it's all part of our routine. No-one has to tell us to get up [unless you are adolescent] or to brush our teeth or go to the toilet. We just do it. It wasn't always that way. As babies we had nappies and an uncontrolled bladder and bowel, no teeth to clean as we suckled milk, no ability to stand, let alone get out of bed and dress ourselves. But as we grew so did our abilities. Our parents taught us the art of using a potty and then a toilet. Our teeth grew so that we could chew food, and our parents introduced us to the toothbrush. We became stronger on our legs and soon cots became beds and we were able to get out of them and started to learn to dress ourselves. Skills were learnt as part of our lifestyle. No-one had to work at them or read books to find out the correct way of brushing our teeth they naturally became part of our lives. Our parents knew what skills we needed at every stage of our development and they gave us opportunity to practice them until we became accomplished, without expecting more than they knew we were capable of. Just as our parents or adults around us helped us to develop physically, so too our heavenly Father knows exactly what skills we need to develop spiritually and how we can get to the point of accomplishing them.

All of those cognitive and physical skills were already programmed into our bodies and our brains at conception. All we had to learn to do was to unlock their potential. Similarly every spiritual gifting is already programmed into us at salvation. All we have to do is learn how to unlock them and their potential. So let's start to look at what we rest in and what our responsibility is.

Imagine you are a blank canvas, nothing on your spiritual map, a new Christian, no pre-conceived ideas just a longing for a relationship with God. Now let's put you in a desert, just you and no-one else but God. He knows you, what kind of learner you are and exactly what you need to develop. You know no different, but as you spend time with Him, the Holy Spirit in your innermost being begins to teach you everything you need to know at the pace and you can handle. All you have to do is rest in the relationship. Tradition says that this was Paul's experience for three years as God laid the foundation for everything Paul would ever be, come up against and ultimately face. God created Paul to be the man of God he became without the aid of a book, DVD or PowerPoint presentation. That time alone with God was the thing that sustained and met every need, and, like Jesus, Paul 'rested' in the relationship both in easy and hard times and could honestly say that God had met his every need even on the road to Rome and in the valley of the shadow of death.

But for us going off for three years, sitting at God's feet, is not an option. For most people reading this you, will have been in a church for some time and will be asking how you can get to that place in God staying where you are right now. Over the next few chapters I hope those answers will come.

You see, just as we trusted with childlike faith the belief that the adults around us knew what we needed to help us use that toothbrush, we need to rest in the knowledge that God just wants to teach us. We need to rely on the fact that He knows what we need to grow and if we allow Him to, He will do the teaching. Now at this moment the cry on some lips will be "How do I know what God is saying?" Well God speaks in a myriad of ways and they are usually personal to you. For those who hear God's voice in the quiet, He will come in the quiet. For those who are loud He will come in the fire but I guarantee that if you put yourself into a place of expectancy and wait, He will speak and He will teach you. If you are in a church that you have peace over being in, then He will speak through your leadership, whether it's your vicar, your pastor, or minister. He will speak through scripture. He will illustrate through nature. He will use every means possible to direct you and show you the abundance of a life lived in Him, because that's all He wants - the relationship with you so that He can teach you and help you be all that you can be in Him.

Some years ago I headed up a youth and children's ministry in quite a hard area and one day I found myself in a local Christian bookshop, determined to buy a resource book by a particular writer who was also heavily into youth ministry in a similar area. As I found the book and reached for it, the Holy Spirit said quite clearly 'Put it back I will teach you' however I picked it up and stood in line to purchase the book even though my heart was pounding and the book (although a simple paperback) felt like lead. Again the Holy Spirit told me to put the book back, and you would think that this time I would listen but, embarrassed by my place in the queue, I stayed put. I now had bright red cheeks to go with the pounding heart and the aching hands with the book being so heavy. I paid for the book and left the shop miserable. Nothing happened until I was 50 yards down the street with my legs also now feeling like lead. This time when the Holy Spirit spoke it was 'Take it back and explain'. I turned around, went back to the shop, stood in line for my refund, and red faced, I explained the reason for the returned book in front of the whole shop. A bemused shopkeeper smiled, refunded the money and I hastily left the shop for the second time, embarrassed but peaceful.

The result was astounding. Our young people and children gave themselves to God empowered by the Spirit. We saw children being used in healings and the prophetic, in ways that we could have only dreamed of. God sat me down, week on week, and showed me what He wanted to teach the children and in three years we never had a generic resource book on our team and we had discipleship groups from 4 years old to 24. Many of them went on to be worship leaders and in full time ministry.

You see God knows you, what makes you tick and what you need. Rest in that and He will direct you to the right church with the right minister with the right teaching for you to be allowed to be helped and released into the furtherance of His kingdom. Maybe it won't be that dramatic but it will be right for you.

The concept of resting in the completeness of God's work, and growth without striving, works when we allow ourselves to let go of the expectations both from our own hearts and others.

We have this idea of being a Christian that has a need to read His word, pray, minister, do church stuff, and be good. The list is endless. Now all of these things are necessary ingredients in our journey with God but if they become a labour of works and not of love they can turn into things that slow down our walk and even cause resentment to form in our hearts. But suppose all we had to do was to wait for the prompting God gave us and then act?

You see that like every good father, and God is the biggest and best, God is more interested in why we do something more than what we do. I have three children. The youngest lives at home, our daughter lives round the corner and our eldest lives further away. Two of my children have their own families with their own demands on their time and their company, and as a parent I can do one of two things, I can either rest in the fact that I know my children love me and that when they can they phone, or come round and we have a fab time together, or I can demand that every day or week I have a visit or a phone call or both because it's what they need to do for me as a parent. My older children do the first of these and I know that when they phone they do it because they want to hear my voice, to find out about my day, share theirs with me, chat through any problems and get some advice, cry, or laugh. They don't do it because of duty or demand; they do it because they want to, and it happens that they do it quite frequently without the pressure of expectation.

God longs for that with us, He doesn't demand we read His Word, pray, do church ministry, or any of the other lists of things that Christians are supposed to do.

He doesn't expect anything from us, or indeed want anything, or even need anything. He just wants to love us and watch us grow. He is more interested (just to reinforce the point) in why we are doing it rather than what we do! And when we do make the space to listen to Him, to read His word, to pray just because we love Him and long to serve Him and our church, it is just so much more precious than doing out of duty.

How different would our spiritual journey look if we rid ourselves of all the expectation and waited for God to grow us in the way He knew was best? If we stopped racing ahead picking up teaching and habits which were not helpful and in fact hindered our growth, causing feelings of failure and dejection what if we did that? You see, we are a fickle people, we always have been and we are very easily taken off track. That coupled with an enemy who is accomplished at knowing our weaknesses causes us real problems. Sometimes the latest teaching that comes out of ministries is good and wholesome and very biblical, but if we take it up without consulting God, and it's not where we or our church is at that time, we can easily get into conflict or start to be manipulated into thinking our leaders are not progressive, or in the extreme that they are wrong by not embracing the latest in evangelizing or prayer or biblical thinking. We must realize that each church (that means the one you are part of) is growing and ministering in their way, in their place, at their pace with their leaders accountable to God. And if the leaders feel that God is taking them in a new direction they will undoubtedly share it.

In Exodus 17 v 21 God led Israel from Egypt onwards to Canaan. He led them by cloud in the day and by fire at night. When either of these stopped, they stopped. When either moved, the people moved. The key to this part of the teaching is that cloud and fire, only moving when God says to move, only praying what God is laying on your heart, reading what the Holy Spirit needs you to learn, helping in the area of church that Gods wants to bless through you and doing it when He asks you to.

If you knew that you were doing exactly what God wanted you to do, when God wanted you to do it and nothing more, if you knew that God had already equipped you with the level of ability needed and time required to achieve what He was asking of you, you would never fail and you never feel a failure, because your responsibility ends with putting yourself in a place where you are listening and waiting on Him. Everything else is His responsibility. He has ordained your life and every day it contains since the beginning of time and He has made it a completed work in Christ.

As I have already touched on problems start to occur when there is an expectation that we put on ourselves to be more than we are, and the expectations we put on others in our fellowships that say they should be trying harder, working more, doing stuff. The result of this is a bitter root which destroys individuals and churches from the inside. (There is more on expectation in the section on Spiritual Healing.)

God expects nothing and hopes for everything based on relationship and love, not on duty and on a false sense of what He requires. Israel had to trust God to take them to Canaan. They had to un-learn a complete way of life that they had lived in Egypt. We too have to make that same journey, to look candidly at why we do things and how we can get to the place of listening to what God wants instead of presuming we know better.

Matt Redman's song 'When the Music fades' was born out of a time when his church stopped "doing" and fell to their knees to discover what it was that God wanted of them. After a lengthy time with no sermons, no worship and only the barest of ministry God gave him the words for that song and it set the church on a new and powerful stage in their corporate walk with God. As individuals 'just because we can, doesn't mean we should' and for some people that discovery of what God wants may mean you letting go of stuff you may have done for years just because you could. As scary as that is, can I assure you that if that is your reality and what you have done is solid silver then God has the gold that He is stretching out in His hand to give you. It also means that He has people in your fellowship or church that He wants to bring on and encourage by giving them the opportunity to do the thing you are holding on to.

We have to learn that God is not interested in failure, He longs for individuals and churches to succeed, but they will only truly reach their potential if they are operating in His rest and following Him. And that may entail some fellowships and churches stopping some ministries completely until God lay on their hearts what He wants them to do.

Jesus used the word "follow" many times, In Mathew 4 v 19 it says *"Come follow me, and I will show you how to fish for people"* In Mark 2 v 14 it says *"Follow me and be my disciple"* In Luke 18 v 43 it says that the instant the blind man was healed he *followed* Jesus praising God and all who saw it praised God too. You see not only are we blessed and grow when we truly follow Jesus doing what He wants us to do and resting in the relationship , but others witnessing it are also blessed and grow. It has a ripple effect in our families, our churches and our communities. Evangelising happens naturally when those around see a people living in peace with themselves and God. Those who are not yet Christians will be drawn far easier to those people than to those who are racing around stressed and worn out. So often we see marriages in conflict because the Christian partner is so busy with church that their non Christian husband/wife is pushed to one side.

Peter writes *"Wives in the same way be submissive to your husbands so that if any of them do not believe the word they may be won over without words by the behaviour of their wives when they see the purity and reverence of your lives"*. [5] Although Peter is writing 'wives' it could easily be the same for a husband. Jesus must never be the competition in a marriage and sadly that is what He becomes when the Christian partner puts church activity over their relationship.

Out of the quality of the relationship we have with God will flow the relationship we have with others both at home, work and with our neighbours. For so many years I put church first, out of a misdirected view of what I thought God wanted. It hurt my family and those around us. Nick and I worked out that at one point we had not had a Sunday off in two years because there was always one person who 'needed' us that week, holidays were taken Sunday night to Saturday and we were always preparing for the sermon during the week. If I could go back and do it again I would guarantee I would do things differently.

But you don't need to be leading a fellowship to put yourselves in that position, with prayer meetings, coffee mornings, outreach, bible study, confirmation classes, alpha, marriage course, town pastors, house groups, deacons meetings, leadership meetings, youth work children's work, lunch clubs, hospital visiting, prison visiting, seminars, teaching days , Sunday mornings, Sunday evenings, quiet days, fun days, prayer walking and many other things that escape me that may be peculiar to your area there is plenty to keep us busy as Christians. And the minister is expected to attend 100% of them in rotation at any given time! Is it any wonder that we are tired of church sometimes? We need to seriously look at what we are responsible for and not try to do everything. Our hearts tell us that we should be

doing and **providing** all of the above but what if God doesn't want us to? Ultimately the biggest and only job that we should be concentrating on is being a disciple of Christ. Out of that flows everything else, so let's turn now to the start of the journey and look at Salvation.

Chapter 3

Salvation

The idea of Salvation is considered important in some denominations but less so in others. Some favour a relationship with God that is devoid of a 'salvation moment'; a specific time when repentance and forgiveness happen, and a relationship with God is born. Others do not consider a person to be a Christian unless that moment has clearly happened in their testimony. So far in this material we have looked at what God's rest is and how it is only true for those who are part of the Christian family; for those who have accepted Jesus as Lord and Saviour of their lives and are now committed to living according to His way and not their own.

As for me, well most of my spiritual journey has been lived under that 'moment' and I, like many others believed wholeheartedly that it was the only way to truly define a believer. That belief also shaped how I thought of those who had yet to commit to a relationship with Jesus and I tasked myself with looking for opportunities to deliver the gospel to anyone who would listen. So do I think differently? Well in essence not really, but the way I view my part in not only my journey but the journey of those around me has definitely changed.

As a general rule we look on Salvation as taking a step of faith. In fact that step is probably the smallest part of what Salvation is.

Let's meet Derek, Derek is your friend and you see him on a regular basis. He is not a Christian but he knows you go to church and, although you don't talk about it much he sees something different in you. One day he expresses an interest in finding out about God. Some people have come to the door talking about heaven and hell and he realised that he doesn't know much. Your church is just about to run a course exploring faith. You tell Derek about it and offer to go with him. He accepts your offer and you do the course together. During that exploration Derek is told the points of salvation, to repent, to accept God's forgiveness, to declare Jesus as Lord, and to accept Him into his life and he responds. You both attend the "Holy Spirit day" and Derek is prayed for to receive the Holy Spirit and is empowered to live the life God has planned for him. From that point on Derek will be encouraged to read his Bible and pray and he will be encouraged to have fellowship in a church where his abilities can be used. What happens next will depend on which fellowship he goes to and the support he receives. One question! At what point did Derek's spiritual journey start? Hold that thought.

In order to understand what our Salvation is, we need to understand as a fundamental fact that it is primarily nothing to do with us. Too much emphasis is put on our response to what is essentially a gift from God. The result of that is that for some people Salvation becomes something to be worked at, with feelings that if we don't live in its fullness we have somehow failed God. And on the surface that idea of 'work' is backed up by scripture.

Paul writes in Philippians 2:12

"Therefore, my dear friends, as you have always obeyed—not only in my presence, but now much more in my absence—continue to **work out your salvation** *with fear and trembling"*. And we do need to work it out, however we either strive in our own strength or understand that the gift of salvation comes with the giver and it is Him who is our strength, resting in God's ability rather than our own allows us to journey with confidence.

If we don't rest in Him instead of entering into a relationship with God which is all He wants, we can enter into a programme of works. As I have said in the previous chapter, God is not so much interested in what we do but why we do it. And it's the same with the gift of salvation, we know that God's heart is that all will be saved and yet He also knows that not all will take up that gift. And countless evangelistic events around the world bear that out, we see vast numbers going forward and repeating the salvation prayer with little evidence of more than a small percentage of those people continuing their journey with God after the event.

In reality Derek, together with you and me, entered into his spiritual journey before his conception. God knew us, and the call to our hearts was already programmed in before we ever took a breath. God has made us a spiritual people, and today in the world around us we see millions reaching out to a wide array of alternative spiritual things to try to fulfil a need in them which is deep in their innermost being.

St Augustine said in the book 'Confessions' "God puts the salt on our lips to make us thirsty" I like that. Salvation is a gift from Him and is always His idea. When God gives us a gift we cannot make it bigger than it is, but equally we cannot make it smaller. Salvation; *Deliverance – (Strongs # 4991)* is His gift to us through Jesus and it is something we just need to accept.

God stirs our interest, He has had our name on His lips for a very long time and He is in no hurry, He knows that at some point that interest will burst into relationship with Him. He puts us in a circle of influence with people who will help in the process of knowing Him just like Derek and you, and then He uses tools like Alpha and others in the process.

"For I know the plans I have for you, plans to prosper you and not to harm you, plans to give you hope and a future." Jeremiah 29 v 11

So why do we feel that salvation is all about the prayer and about the words we say? As I have touched upon so many are taken to meetings or put on courses that give a call at some point to enter into a relationship with God. Are they wrong? Of course not, but I would again ask the question why we are sometimes fixated with our response to a salvation moment.

There needs to be a spiritual awakening which God prompts. In John 3 v 1-21 we see Nicodemus coming to Jesus at night to find out more about this preacher from Galilee who had stated that He was the Son of God. In the discourse he asked Jesus for explanations of the things he had personally witnessed, acknowledging at the same time that they could only have been done by someone who God was obviously with. Jesus answered with an explanation of the gospel and a clear call to be saved. We do not have the privilege of reading Nicodemus' response to the words that Jesus said to him but later on in Johns Gospel (John 19 v 39) we read that alongside Joseph of Arimathea, Nicodemus was there at Jesus tomb with the burial spices of myrrh and aloes. So it is safe to say that although we have no 'salvation moment' documented for Nicodemus, God had salted his lips enough to bring him to the point of openly being involved with the burial of our Saviour and into relationship with the other disciples around. We can with a fair amount of certainty conclude that from that point on it would have been those relationships which would have determined what happened next to Nicodemus and, who knows, perhaps he was one of the 120 disciples that waited patiently in that upper room when the Holy Spirit fell in awesome power?

So then how does 'Rest' fit in with Salvation? To examine this we need to look at the relationship between God and man. What it was and where we are now.

In Eden God wanted the best for Adam, and He gave him everything he needed to have a complete life with Eve. All Adam had to do was to rest in what he had been given and, to be fair, for a while he did that, and he bathed in the relationship that allowed God to walk by his side in the garden He had created. However Adam, as we know, chose to want more and that cost him everything. Thrown from God's presence, both Adam and Eve were left to provide for themselves. In the harshest environment they had to work for every scrap of food, clothing and comfort that they got from that moment on. Through Jesus, all that Adam had lost was restored to us, but in order for us to live the life God wants us to have we need to learn to truly rest in what Jesus gives us in the gift of Salvation.

So what does this gift contain? Firstly it gives us relationship. Up to the point where we acknowledge our need of God, repent and accept this gift of Salvation, we have no relationship with Him at all. We can have a belief in God without a relationship and that feels a comfortable place to be for some folk, because it allows them to be unaccountable for their actions. They can work for Him and for the church but not really have the commitment or need to engage in His ways or purposes.

Relationship requires closeness, accountability, good communication and time to grow. "Love at first sight" is really a myth in my opinion; love develops over time so that it becomes strong enough to withstand the hurricane of things that are there to test the partnership.

God's relationship with us has been there since before our conception but our part in that relationship is much younger. It takes time to feel confident in knowing when He is speaking to us, directing us or perhaps disciplining us. However none of that is even possible unless we have accepted this love gift in the first place and stand in the benefit of His salvation promises.

True relationship is two way; it doesn't demand that one side gives more than the other although at different times one partner will for a variety of reasons give the extra bit. It commits itself and always wants the best for each other. God's relationship with us is no different, He knows that we can never give the same to Him as He does to us (although some of us try hard) but still lavishes all that He can to our wellbeing and provision.

Salvation is not just what we have, it is our position, and it's who we are. In John Jesus says *"I am the vine, you are the branches. He who abides in Me, and I in him, bears much fruit; for without Me you can do nothing"* [6] He is dedicated to this relationship and to its growth in Him. A relationship based on anything other than love will always be a shadow of what it could be.

Secondly the gift of Salvation gives deliverance. It means that sin is no longer in control; we have choice and power over it. So many Christians feel that they are weak and unable to control their sinful habits but the reality is far from that point. Let's go to our blueprint model again; Jesus.

When Jesus walked away from His baptism and into the desert it was the 'prequel' to the cross. Satan knew that if he could get Jesus to falter at this point it would all be over, the three temptations Satan brought to the table are fundamentally the same that he comes to us with so we should note Jesus response.

Firstly Jesus fasted for 40 days. Fasting and the focus it brought Jesus was a key element to Him overcoming Satan's scheme. In Mathew we read about a boy needing deliverance ministry. Jesus' disciples had prayed for the boy and nothing had changed so he had been brought to Jesus who immediately rebuked the demon and delivered the boy. The disciples then went privately to Jesus, not understanding their lack of power in the situation, and Jesus says this *"Because of your unbelief; for assuredly I say to you if you have faith as a mustard seed you will say to this mountain 'move from here to there' and it will move; and nothing will be impossible for you However, this kind does not go out except by prayer and fasting"*[7]. Here you see Him addressing the disciple's lack of belief in their ability, but acknowledges that when faced with the demonic, fasting gives an extra and vital dynamic to the situation.

By fasting in the wilderness He was not just having a break from food, He was honing in on the added spiritual power that fasting gives. He knew that this was one of two key times that Satan would seek to derail Him and He wanted to be prepared. Remember we are not talking about the 'fully God' bit of Jesus who Satan has to bow the knee to, but we are looking at the 'fully man' bit of Jesus which was much more vulnerable. As the 40 days comes to a close, although his physical body was weakened, his spiritual body was strong. This event came on the heels of His baptism and a time when all scripture had been fulfilled. It was at this point that Satan comes with the first temptation.

He didn't lay a banquet before Jesus to tempt Him to eat because the temptation, although an attack on His physical being, was much deeper than that. *"If you are the Son of God command this stone to become bread" Luke 4 v 3.* So Satan challenged Jesus' position as well as tempting Him to use that position to feed Himself and to ease the hunger His physical body was feeling. Jesus counteracted immediately with the one thing that Satan cannot argue against: God's Word, and He quotes Deuteronomy 8 v3 *"Man shall not live on bread alone but by every word of God"*. It's not that Jesus wasn't hungry, Luke 4 v 2 says that He was, but during that time of fasting and praying in the desert alone God had commissioned Him and nothing was going to sway His focus.

So, thwarted by the word of God, Satan tried again. This time he took Jesus to a high mountain and offered the whole of the world's authority and wealth to Him, if He would only worship him. The book of Revelation [8] tells us that indeed this authority had been given to him and therefore it was his to give away. This temptation comes against the spiritual authority that Jesus had, because worship is indeed giving worth to something or someone of great spiritual authority. Satan had tried it before in the throne room of heaven and it's what got him kicked out in the first place. Again Jesus counteracted, not with His own thoughts or words, but with God's word from Deuteronomy 10 v 20 *"You shall worship the Lord your God and Him only you shall serve"* It was enough to send Satan away for a second time.

Then he came a third time in a final effort to tempt Jesus. He took Him to the top of the temple in Jerusalem, a feat within itself demonstrating the power Satan has here on earth. He then challenged Jesus to throw Himself off and quoted scripture from Psalm 91 v 11 to back it up *"He shall give His angels charge over you, to keep you........... In their hands they shall bear you up, lest you dash your foot against a stone"*. This was the most devious temptation; if Jesus refused to throw Himself off He could be accused of not believing the scripture was either true or even about Him. If He does throw himself down Satan has won anyway. Either way the 'accuser' looked set for a victory. Again Jesus stood His ground and quoted back from scripture

Deuteronomy 6 v 16 *"You should not tempt the Lord your God"* and Satan left.

We close this account reading that Jesus returned in the power of the Spirit to Galilee to begin His three year journey to the cross.

So Jesus withstood challenges and temptations over His physical wellbeing, His spiritual position and His authority. The same Holy Spirit power is who you and I have living inside of us. There is nothing that we are tempted with that does not fall under one of these categories and like Jesus we need to understand and implement the tools which will counteract any spiritual attack when it comes. Sometimes we just need to stand on His word knowing that no power or authority can stand against it. Other times we may need to fast and pray knowing that if God is calling us to fast he will equip us with the means not to fail.

The truth is that we have, through Jesus, a salvation promise that delivers us from the control of sin and enables us to stand against 'every temptation'. And that changes things for us. It means that we **are** empowered to live the life God wants for us. It is no longer impossible. But it is in our humanity that sometimes we choose not to.

Thirdly salvation gives us authority. It gives us authority over sickness, creation, the powers and principalities of this world and sin. It is a fact that every Christian has that authority to command but we don't use it to full advantage, and some of us don't even believe it but I can guarantee you that as a Christian no matter what you have been told, **you have authority**, and it is the same authority that Jesus had on earth. Everything He did you can do.

When Jesus came to earth he lived as you or I might have done. It is only when we read the account of the temptation that we really see the first glimpses of anything extraordinary and by that time He was thirty years old. When Jesus moved in the power of the Holy Spirit He did as much as we can today, an incredible statement to make but to validate it we need to believe what Jesus said in the statement at the beginning of this book; that you and I would do immeasurably more than He did.

Throughout His ministry we see Him taking authority over sickness, healing person after person, and that is just the healing stories that were recorded. We see Him bringing children and adults back from the dead and reuniting families. On the water He tames nature bringing calm to the Sea of Galilee, a notoriously difficult water to read even by the men that fished it. In spiritual battle He counteracted demons, sending them scurrying away as He commanded them to leave their human targets. And as we have just seen in the desert He combated the temptation to sin very efficiently.

He sends the first disciples out in Luke *"Then He called His twelve disciples together and gave them power and authority over all demons, and to cure diseases. He sent them to preach the kingdom of God and to heal the sick"*[9]

In Luke again Jesus says this *"Behold I give you the authority to trample on serpents and scorpions and over all the power of the enemy, and nothing shall by any means hurt you"*[10]

In the book of John Jesus tells us *" However when He the Spirit of truth has come He will guide you into all truth; for He will not speak on His own authority, but whatever He hears He will speak; and He will tell you things to come. He will glorify Me, for He will take hold of what is mine and declare it to you. All things that the Father has are Mine. Therefore I said that He will take of Mine and declare it to you."*[11]

When the Holy Spirit came that first Pentecost and empowered those first disciples He brought about a chain reaction that has been a fact ever since: Those who take hold of the gift of Salvation receive the authority of heaven to combat all that would stand in the way of kingdom living.

The enemy will lie, trick and cheat his way into getting you to believe something different or tell you that all of that was for then and not for now. Don't listen! His objective, as it was for Jesus, is to keep you from fulfilling the purposes of God and being a bright light in this dark world. If that has been you, repent, be forgiven, and begin to stand in the authority that you have.

Lastly we have an Inheritance. Salvation gives us the same inheritance as Jesus, and the knowledge that at the end of our earthly lives we will go to His side. Inheritance is something that some struggle with because it implies that we are worthy and that is a problem for those who feel less than precious. Well it's a good job that God doesn't measure us on the same scale as we do because through the acceptance of this gift of salvation we automatically become worthy and entitled to full inheritance status.

We share Jesus' inheritance over the physical world. God created all things living through Him, by Him and for His glory, the Genesis world of purity and love, complete in Christ. Man was commissioned as its custodian and we know the mess we have made of it ever since, however in Revelation we read of the restoration of a perfect world. A new heaven and new earth appear and the old pass away and God once again dwells with man [12]. In Christ we will share in that, at this present time it is not complete but one day we will have our feet firmly planted on an earth that our Saviour stands on once again.

Secondly we have a Spiritual inheritance. In 1 Peter it says this *"....to an inheritance incorruptible and undefiled and that does not fade away reserved in heaven for you, who are kept by the power of God through faith for salvation ready to be revealed in the last time"*[13]. Paul writes in Ephesians [14] that we are, through salvation, sealed with the Holy Spirit of promise who is a guarantee of our inheritance. The Holy Spirit is a down payment of the fullness of that spiritual inheritance that we will receive in heaven, because it is only there when we are free from the restraints of sin that we are able to fully partake in all that God has for us.

Back in Exodus the inheritance that Israel was walking towards was Canaan, for us that earthly place is now a spiritual place; a place of God's rest. Both our physical and spiritual inheritance culminates in our being with God for eternity. However in the lead up to those exciting days we can partake of all that living in Him truly means.

There is a principle that God applies to every gift that He gives us, starting with Salvation, and it is the principle of opportunity. As soon as He can, as we grow He puts before us opportunity to know Him, He begins to touch our lives with His, through creation, emotion, our senses and knowledge. He begins a courtship of love gently showing us who He is, we may not have a name for Him, we may not understand the salt crystals forming on our lips, but at various points along the way He will give us opportunity to get to know Him as God. *"For I know the plans I have for you"* As He does this, and yes it's all coming from Him, at some point in some way we take that big opportunity. It may be on an Alpha course or in a meeting or in your back garden but it will always happen just at the right time for you. For me it happened in our vicar's house as we were kneeling in prayer at the end of a question and answer session. I told God that He had to come and kick my backside because if I felt it, then I would believe it. This surge of power which is the only word I can use to describe it hit the top of my head and travelled to my feet. When I got up, I knew that God was there with me. No-one had told me about the prayer of salvation but I knew I had been saved that day. Two weeks later at a Billy Graham meeting in my home town I knelt again and said the prayer of salvation with countless others and in tears knew God had completed the call He had started in me at the beginning of my life.

It should never be about the right words to say, or the right order in which to pray. Sometimes it's just 'O God help! Yes, in my opinion we need to repent, yes we need to accept this wonderful gift of salvation and Jesus coming into our lives and yes, we need to be forgiven but God will deal with all of that. Sometimes He comes to us just as He did with me and the words come later, because it's never a formula with God it's a relationship. The best relationships are ones which are naturally formed and naturally grow. God's relationship with us is no exception. Once we have started to respond to Him we find ourselves seeking His company more regularly. Prayer becomes a time where we communicate with Him and Him with us. We find ourselves eager to find out more about Him by reading His Word. All of these things are down to God building the relationship and then giving us opportunity to respond *"Plans to prosper you and not to harm you"* Operating in God's rest allows this to happen in the way God intended. Some of us who feel guilty when our lives crowd into our "God time" will be released when we start to respond to God's prompting and opportunity rather than operate in works because that is what we think we 'should be' doing. God will always lead us to a fertile place of fellowship and surround us with godly people in order for us to have the maximum opportunities to grow in Him, but only if we let Him.

If we are only doing what God says when He says it we will be privileged to see Him work out other people's spiritual journeys together with ours *"plans to give you hope and a future"*. Then as God prompts us we will start to pray for others, praying things that God puts into our hearts and minds. We will say the things He wants us to say at the right time, and suddenly the pressure will be off. We will not feel responsible for the gospel, for providing courses or anything else and we will not feel responsible for getting it right every time. God never intended the great commission in Mathew 28 v 19 to be a lead weight around our necks, something to be worked at because Jesus commanded it. This wonderful commission **is** ours but only in partnership with God, we are not on our own in this. God will show our leaders in our fellowships what they are to offer in outreach and if we feel God is calling us to be a part of it then great, jump in with both feet, but if God is calling you to befriend someone, to make the teas, to clear the chairs or to gently speak kind words when prompted, if you are that person it is of no less value than those who stand in stadiums and speak to the masses.

God is calling us to rest every aspect of our spiritual life in Him, to move with Him and enjoy our relationship and our salvation journey. We can only do that if we shed the responsibility for it and move in the opportunity of it.

Chapter 4

Faith

Someone once gave me a plaque as a gift and it reads 'Faith is not believing God can it is knowing He will'. Well as blessed by the gift as I was, circumstances happened in our lives when it felt that as much as I believed God could, He didn't. And I know that there are many of you who are out there having lost loved ones even though you prayed and had 'faith' for their healing that feel much the same.

For this chapter it would help if you read the book of *Hebrews 11 1- 6. And Hebrews 12 1-2*

These verses are probably some of the most quoted in scripture on Faith and they are wonderfully phrased; *"Faith is the substance of things hoped for the evidence of things not seen"*

Up until God started teaching me about resting in what He had done for me I had always thought of Faith as being what I believed in spiritually. Now I know that it is something completely different. We can believe all we like but if something is not there it really doesn't matter how much I believe it is the truth will tell me otherwise. So we can only conclude that Faith is not what we believe.

So what is it? I would like us to consider this in depth and to do that we must once again go back to the previous chapter and look again at Derek.

Long before Derek got to the point of asking you about God, long before the people had turned up at his door God stirred something deep within him. *"Now faith is the substance of things **hoped** for"*[15], the important word here is hoped. You see miles before we are saved, God stirs up hope, and sometimes it catches us unawares. Things happen and we find ourselves hoping there is more to life and death than a void, a way out, someone who is bigger than us and can help share the burden. It's that hope that is the catalyst for what happens next, and like everything else it comes from God.

So Derek has for some time hoped that there was something more. Eventually as we discovered a few pages back he is brought into a situation where the gospel of Jesus and His message of salvation is shared. At some point something clicks in Derek's heart and that hope gives birth to belief, he hears the gospel and makes the human decision to believe what he is hearing. But it's not over yet, because at the moment when hope births belief, God births faith.

Faith is one of the most powerful gifts God gives us, but it is a gift that cannot be shared with those outside God's family it is only available to those folk who have accepted God's gift of salvation. Up to the point of salvation we can only operate in human belief and trust, we cannot operate in faith. And that is why many thousands of churchgoing folk as dear as they are, will still only be able to live their spiritual journey in belief and not faith because to access the power of faith you must bow the knee and submit to the Lordship of Christ, entering into His family and His salvation promises. And that is why the gospel must be preached in its entirety without compromise.

Like every gift that God gives us, we cannot add to it and make it bigger nor can we take anything away from it and make it smaller. Jesus tells us that faith as small as a mustard seed can move a mountain and we see, in some parts of the world, faith operating on that scale. They may be mountains of sickness, poverty and death and not ones of rock and stone but they still make some of us look longingly and ask ourselves how we get that kind of faith?

If faith comes from God and is His gift to us, it stands to reason that He alone knows how much of it we can handle. He would not, as a loving Father, give faith in great measure to someone whose lifestyle cannot contain it or use the gift with proper care. That would be like giving a high performance car to a learner driver. The likelihood is that it would end up seriously debilitating them, if not killing them spiritually.

God gifts us according to where we are. If faith to really 'move mountains'[16] were given to someone whose spiritual character was underdeveloped he/she could end up moving in pride or worse over the effect of 'their ministry'. Sadly we have seen the result of this across several 'revival' spots in the world where seemingly staggering miracles have been witnessed only to be discovered as highly exaggerated at a later date. The chances are that if someone is making a great show of what God is doing through them it won't last long and will be proven to have an ulterior motive. God sits with humble hearts. He can never sit on the same bench as sin, He will never bless those who are walking in it unrepentant and proud and it will eventually be proved false and worthless.

Peter and John came up against the sorcerer Simon in the book of Acts;

"But there was a certain man called Simon, who had previously practiced sorcery in the city and astonished the people of Samaria, claiming that he was someone great, to whom they gave heed, from the least to the greatest, saying 'This man is the great power of God'. And they heeded him because he had astonished them with his sorceries for a long time"[17]

And further on

"...prayed for them that they might receive the Holy Spirit for as yet He had fallen upon none of them. They had only been baptized in the name of the Lord Jesus. Then they laid hands on them and they received the Holy Spirit. And when Simon saw that through the laying on

of the apostles hands the Holy Spirit was given, he offered them money saying ' Give me this power also that anyone whom I lay hands may receive the Holy Spirit.' But Peter said to him 'Your money perish with you because you thought that the gift of God could be purchased with money! You have neither part or portion in this matter for your heart is not right in the sight of God'." [18]

The first thing we see in this passage is that Simon claimed that he was someone great, and even though he had given up sorcery and had believed the preaching of Philip when he came to the area, he was still operating in self mode. He also thought that the gifts of God were up for barter and offered Peter money in return for him to be able to lay hands on the people to receive the gift of the Holy Spirit. In response Peter, the rough former fisherman whose manner and demeanour were not as polished as the courts usually demanded put Simon in his place by declaring that he had no part or portion in their ministry because his heart was so far away from where it should have been.

Before we nod self righteously at this story I would ask that you look again because it is possible that, if God has used us in the past, there was a small part of us that enjoyed it and the recognition that it brought, whether it was in prayer, in prophecy or in preaching. We are all vulnerable to those feelings because they play on our sense of worth to God.

We may not have actually offered money in return for greater influence than we already have, but some of us have at some point bartered with 'works' for power or influence. How many of us can identify with prayers that have included "Lord if I fast and pray please let me used for you to bring healing to this situation".

If you are a Christian who has committed your life to the service of Christ have repented and submitted to the Lordship of Christ you can be assured that God has given you the right amount of faith that you need right now, and you don't need another ounce more to do what He wants you to do.

So does that stop us from asking for more faith? Certainly not! In 1 Corinthians 12 v 9 Paul tells us to earnestly seek the gifts of God and faith is one of the biggest. But alongside our seeking we should be allowing God to shape our whole character in order to provide a lifestyle compatible with that increased faith.

In Hebrews 11 it says *"Without faith it is impossible to please Him, for he who comes to God must believe that He is and that He is a rewarder of those who diligently seek Him"*[19]

If we earnestly seek God's face [who He is] rather than His hand [what He can give], resting in everything He has done and not trying to get better at things on our own, we will begin to learn of God and His way of doing things. In turn this will draw us closer to Him and then asking God to give us opportunity to grow our faith will, when taken advantage of see our faith grow.

So what happens if we don't take advantage of the opportunity when He gives it to us, what happens then? The short answer is nothing, we won't grow our faith, but it won't diminish, the size of the gift stays the same as it was before you had the opportunity.

"But I have lost my faith!" you cry....no, you cannot lose the gift God has given you. He is the only one who can take it back and He doesn't do that [more about gifts in the next chapter]. You may have lost a bit of belief because belief is a human attribute, but faith is a God thing and it will always belong to you. The more you exercise it the more it grows, but if you don't exercise it, it stays the same. How do we know that? Going back to the verses in Hebrews it says *"....and that He is a rewarder of those who diligently seek Him"*[20]. God rewards us with increase as we seek Him and His ways to grow us into the people of God He has destined us to be. And that applies to every gift He has given including faith.

For years some of us have beaten ourselves up as to why we are unable to live the way God wants us to. We have pleaded with Him to let us see the miracles that are seemingly happening everywhere else but here. Finally we can start to see that faith is this wonderful gift and not some attribute that we should strive to get better at. And we can relax in the knowledge that we have exactly the correct amount that God knows we can handle right at this moment in time.

As we understand in a deeper way that everything comes from Him in the measure that is right for us we will no longer look longingly at others trying to get the measure of faith they seem to have. Instead included in our daily prayers will be;

"Lord thank you for the measure of faith that you have given me. Today give me an opportunity to use that faith, and as I use, it let it grow.

So, if faith is a gift from God, given for us to use in the Kingdom of God, then what about the other gifts He has given and how do we provide a lifestyle worthy of increase?

Chapter 5

Gifts and the Fruit of the Spirit

[Lifestyle and Increase]

Galatians 5 v 16-26

'Walk in the Spirit'. It is easy to think that this is something we should do rather than something we should be, after all walking involves the effort to get out of the chair in the first place. But as with all the things of God if we examine it, we shall see that this is not what it first seems.

When we start to think of spiritual gifts we immediately think of the list in 1 Corinthians 12 v 4-11 ; Wisdom, knowledge, faith, healing, miracles, discerning of spirits, tongues, interpretation of tongues. Further on in this chapter Paul adds apostles, teachers, helps and administrations to those gifts. He then goes on to say that in his opinion the greatest of the gifts is none of the above, but is love and then he follows on telling us what love really is.

The fruit of the Spirit which in essence is exhibited when we are moving in the gifts of the spirit is found in Galatians 5 v 22 ; Love, joy, peace, patience, kindness, goodness, faithfulness, gentleness, and self control. The two go hand in hand. If we are living in the fullness of the Spirit, allowing God to have full access to our lives then not only will He use us in the kingdom of God but we will also exhibit the fruit of the Spirit. On paper it seems so simple.

In the chapter on Faith we have seen how God takes us on a voyage of discovery in Him from the very beginning and how when we move into belief He gives us faith and everything else we need for rest of the journey. It is clear that as we walk with Him we will have the ability to use those gifts as appropriate to what God is asking of us at any one particular time.

Sadly some will look at the first passage in 1 Corinthians 12 and decide that these gifts are something they need to obtain, much as we saw Simon in the previous chapter trying to barter for the ability to lay hands on believers for baptism of the Spirit. But as well as trying to obtain these gifts others will look at Galatians 5 and see a list of the 'proof's that we are walking in the Spirit [or not]? Perhaps we need to look again and to see instead the hope of Christ for us as He disciples us into the men and women of God He wants us to be.

We have previously looked at how God will not gift us with anything in a measure that our lifestyle cannot contain; starting with faith. This is also true of every other gift that He has for us, so it stands to reason that before we can examine the gifts of the Spirit we need to first look at the fruit of the Spirit and our lifestyles.

Paul says in Galatians 21 that if we walk in the Spirit we will not fulfil the lusts of the flesh; well we all know that one. The flesh and the Spirit life are at war with each other and are constantly pulling in opposite directions for our attention. Further on in this passage Paul lists some of the 'flesh' things that we battle with every day and you can always count on our enemy to make sure that we do. Our humanity will always battle with our spirit life, it's not that we are weak or evil it's simply the nature of self.

God gives us every part of Himself that He can share. Through His Spirit we can tap into a supernatural way of living, utilising every gift and exhibiting the fruit of the Spirit as we do so. So why is it that we find ourselves struggling so much? When the Holy Spirit takes up residence in us our fleshly 'normal' spirit reacts. Just like our physical body tries to oust an infection, so our flesh life tries to push against the Holy Spirit egged on by temptation and all the rest of the enemy's weapons. The result is an ongoing battle of monumental proportion. The good news is that our flesh life won't win the battle. "God in us" is too strong so we can never lose our salvation. However, the choices we make will hamper us from fully tapping into the strength that God gives us by His Spirit to live the life He longs for us to have and to fully take hold of the gifts with which He has already empowered us.

Even St Paul battled with his self- life, stating in Romans *" For what I am doing, I do not understand. For what I will to do, that I do not practice; but what I hate, that I do"*[22] The Message puts it like this *" What I don't understand about myself is that I decide one way, but then I act another, doing things I absolutely despise".* I am positive that this resonates with all of us and surely if such a man of God filled with the Spirit and walking so closely with God struggled then should we not expect the same? Of course we should, the battle doesn't cease. In this passage Paul encourages us by truthfully admitting that he found life difficult at times, and as much as we have learnt that through salvation we are no longer under the control of sin, we still have the ability to choose to be sinful.

In Gethsemane Jesus calls out in desperation and fear. In Luke 22 it says *"Father, if it is your will take this cup away from me; nevertheless not My will but Yours be done". Then an angel appeared to Him from heaven, strengthening Him*[23]'. It may be controversial to say that Jesus was afraid but we see Him asking His disciples in Mathew [24] to watch with Him as His soul was exceedingly sorrowful. If indeed the 'fully man' Jesus experienced all of life's challenges it stands to reason that fear would be amongst them. I believe He did experience fear on that night, perhaps not just of the physicality of what was about to happen, but also fear of the separation from the Father that it would bring. That thought was so horrendous to Jesus that it records in Luke [25] Him asking for the cup of suffering to be taken away.

Our enemy has an unrelenting desire to keep us from our full inheritance in God and he will use every trick in the book to get us off track. Jesus knew what lay ahead and His humanity wobbled, but His Spirit life; that relationship with Father God rested in God's will, and His humanity followed. *"...not My will but Yours be done*[25]. It is right at this point that we can clearly see Jesus separating one from the other; His will and God's. It tells us that they were different, that right at that moment He did not, in His humanity, want to face the cross with the pain, loss, and rejection that it would bring. But it also gives us clarity on His earthly life living and resting in Gods will and bidding. It reassures us that even in a situation where we could be called to give our lives God will always come through, strengthening us and keeping us close to Him. It shows us what a life resting in God can be like. As Christians, for the most part, we battle every day to try to do the right thing, say the right thing and be better at living the Christian life. Here we see the ultimate example of what it means to give ourselves over to Gods way of doing things and let Him lead us in our daily walk.

There is a wide gap between what our responsibility is and what God's is and when we get hold of what the difference is then our whole lives will change. As I have said before it is not that we do nothing, but what we do must run parallel to what God is asking us to do. Paul writes in Colossians *"To this end I also labour, striving according to **His** working [action/operating power] which works in me mightily"*[26].

When we are the deciding voice on what we do in our lives we will only be operating in our own strength and that not only limits us, it puts in a very vulnerable position. So, if trying to be the people that we want to be doesn't work, then how do we become more Christ like?

When John the Baptist was asked about Jesus as He walked away into the desert from His baptism he says in John 3 *"He must increase I must decrease"*[27]. This is one of the most powerful prophetic statements in the New Testament and it is a vital key for us to unlock the full potential of Gods gifts in our lives.

The Holy Spirit [Jesus] must increase and when He does, your flesh life [you/me] will naturally decrease. In order for the Holy Spirit to maximise the impact He has in our life we need Him to access every area. We will effectively decrease as He touches our life with His. In the end the "flesh" withers not because we 'try' not to do the things that are wrong, it withers because we rest in what **God** is doing in us, responding to His bidding and His timing.

He alone truly knows you and He knows the sins, habits and shortcomings that are part of your life, and He is a God of order. So often we examine ourselves [not wrong], but then instead of handing over the problem to God and believing the fact that a heartfelt repentance will bring God's forgiveness and His strengthening, we take over and with steely determination we vow not to do it again. The result of this is weeks, months or even years of working at it until one day we do, do it again and then feel absolute failures.

In 1 Timothy Paul calls for Timothy to be diligent, he said this

"Watch your life and doctrine closely. Persevere in them, because if you do, you will save both yourself and your hearers"[28]. We are called to be diligent in our faith, we need to keep short account and to ask for and give forgiveness readily. And we need to persevere, not give up on our faith journey. However all of this is impossible to do long term if we don't allow ourselves into Gods hands, His timing and His ways.

Sin for the most part doesn't stand alone; there is always a reason behind it. I am not saying there is an excuse that is a wrong way of thinking; reason and excuse are diametrically opposed to each other when talking about sin. But a thread can often be traced back, some call this the root and it is biblical to think of it as such. Roots are hidden things in the natural world as well as in the spiritual realm and our enemy likes to keep them that way. It doesn't pay him to allow the roots of sin to be seen because if they are exposed then we can deal with them.

The trouble with physical roots in a garden is that you can cut off the top of the shrub and get rid of the evidence but eventually new growth starts to spring up and poke its way through the soil. The only way to get rid of the plant is to dig it up or kill the root, both take effort. The other thing to take on board is that when you do start digging around very often you chop away at the root system, cutting through bit by bit until all that's left is the taproot; the main root that has been sent deep into the earth. It's only when this is cut that you find you are able to rid yourself of the plant.

We operate in the same way. We can have good folk help us to take the top off our sinful acts/attitudes in prayer, and we can suppress the new growth that will undoubtedly come but unless that root is truly dealt with we will never be free and we will use endless amounts of 'spiritual' energy trying not to let the growth poke through into our Christian lives. How much easier is accepting the fact that we are a 'work in progress' and that if we are content to allow God to work in His time we will see the smaller roots dealt with one by one, in His order, until the taproot is exposed and chopped off. Then the sinful act /attitude can be lifted away from our lives and we become more like Jesus. If we keep hold of the responsibility for changing ourselves then we will battle with sin forever, and that is contrary to what God wants for us. I am not saying that resting in God means that we will be sin free, but the responsibility for bringing about that change becomes God's and if we allow Him to do it then it will happen a lot faster and more effectively than when we take it on personally.

So allowing God to change us at the pace and with the content He knows is right for us gives us a major breakthrough in our attitude and our walk with Him and also our expectation of others, but it's always our choice. Our enemy is committed to keeping us from this freedom, he will tell us over and over again to do it ourselves, because that way he keeps us in a loop of failure; don't allow it! Turn from self sufficiency to God sufficiency and break free.

Church can be a minefield of expectation, and it's not surprising. If we expect so much from ourselves then we are bound to transfer that expectation to those around us, and they don't disappoint. Why should they, after all they are in the same position, trying to sort out their lives with minimal help from Father God who must be saddened by our actions. Why have we got this mantle of responsibility? The truth is we are born with it, passed on to each generation together with our sinful nature. Self rises up in us with independence at its heel, and makes us dig ourselves into an attitude that says it is our problem to solve. **No it is not! It is Gods.**

Our children are wonderful and their lives are full of peaks and troughs just like ours. When things are going well we celebrate with them. When things go badly we stand with them and do whatever we can to help them sort it out. Imagine finding out your child was struggling with debt, or drugs, or that they had stolen or hurt someone. Imagine them going through that trough alone, struggling in court, or in an alley huddled over their addiction. The first words that you would say are "Why didn't you tell me?" because although you might not be able to make the result of their actions go away, at least they would not be going through the pain alone. And that is all we need to do, to go to God, tell Him and then ask Him to help. As He responds and you listen He will direct you, cut through each root that binds you and set you free.

Jesus said in John 8 *"Therefore if the Son makes you free, you shall be free indeed"* [29]. If we accept God's gift of Salvation and truly allow God to build our relationship with Him then we will be free to live and move in the gifts that He has through Salvation already empowered us with.

So what have we learnt?

Firstly we know that we are gifted with everything we need from the day of salvation, as Paul writes in 1 Corinthians *" Therefore you do not lack any spiritual gift as you eagerly await Lord Jesus"*[30] . And as we listen to Him we will have the ability to use those gifts when He wants us to.

Secondly the gifting will be at the right level for us; it won't be too hard and it won't take up more time than we can cope with.

Thirdly it will come as a result of us listening to and building our relationship with God, not out of trying to impress Him and others around us.

Lastly we will stop looking at the Galatians list as a spiritual temperature guide as to whether we and those around us are 'good enough' Christians.

Those of us who are still operating in a work based relationship with God end up living in a loop of trying, failing, trying and failing. Our walk with God is fraught with feelings of despondency and desperation to use the gifts God has given to us for some kind of validation. And before we start to think about people who are in that place I can tell you without a shadow of a doubt that we have all been there or are there. We need to feel useful, we need to feel that our gifts are being used and we try hard to prove to people around us that we are worthy of that process by exhibiting all the right attributes. Truthfully, just to make the point again, if we actually knew that every gift was in us to 100% capacity, and if we were living in what God has already done, then we would also know that the gifting He needs to be used by us, would be used, in the way He wants it to be used, when He wants it to be used, where He wants it to be used and nothing can limit that happening, except us.

In Romans 12 Paul writes a passage on humility and grace, teaching the church that no gift should be thought of as higher than another;

"For by the grace given me I say to every one of you: Do not think of yourself more highly than you ought, but rather think of yourself with sober judgment, in

accordance with the faith God has distributed to each of you. For just as each of us has one body with many members, and these members do not all have the same function, so in Christ we, though many, form one body, and each member belongs to all the others. We have different gifts, according to the grace given to each of us. If your gift is prophesying, then prophesy in accordance with your faith; if it is serving, then serve; if it is teaching, then teach; if it is to encourage, then give encouragement; if it is giving, then give generously; if it is to lead, do it diligently; if it is to show mercy, do it cheerfully"[31]

Paul teaches that as a body of people we will see a variety of gifts used at different times and that we should not be envious of anyone else. We should use the gift graciously understanding that it is God who has given it to us. This passage does not say we have one individual gift to be used, we are **all called** to give, to encourage, to serve, and to be merciful. In truth there will some folk who are especially gifted to teach, and there are those whom God has set aside to be in leadership. All of the gifts are distributed by the Holy Spirit as He determines in accordance with His will, to enrich and empower the churches ministry.

You may ask how scripture seems at odds with itself. In 1 Corinthians 1:7 Paul clearly says that we do not lack any spiritual gift, whereas 1 Corinthians 12 seems to speak of individuals being gifted in one way. I believe that both are correct; that we are filled with every spiritual gift as we give ourselves in relationship to God, but that the Holy Spirit does raise a particular gift in us at different times to be used to glory God and for the furtherance of His Kingdom.

By now we are beginning to grasp the principles of rest and how they permeate every aspect of our spiritual walk. We are starting to understand that God gives us opportunities to exercise the gifts that He has given us and that as we exercise them He develops them, just like faith in the previous chapter. But that's not all that happens. As those gifts develop, we develop. As we begin to listen to God we begin to hear Him, to move with Him, to live in Him. He increases and we decrease. Suddenly, the more we rest, the more we move. The less we try, the more we grow. As we take our hands off, His hands move on. This is the simplicity of displacement. No longer are we living in the 'should be' law we are living in the 'Rest of God'. Our days are filled with moving in Him, watching for His prompting and taking hold of the opportunities of exercising the gifts He has lavished on us.

Imagine, if you will, a people no longer saying "I have the gift of healing" or "I have the gifting of the prophetic" but saying "I have every gift that God has for me". So often church is working with people who think that God has one ministry or one area of service for them. Truthfully God may be using them in a particular area at that time but it is their mindset that limits them to that, not God. You see God wants a people who can be used in many areas of service to Him and their fellowship. Maybe Derek will be used in a prayer of healing today, but if he is open to God, tomorrow God may use him in an entirely different way. We need to open our hearts to God and allow Him to not only bless others through our service to them but be blessed ourselves.

There is a danger that we may limit what God can do through us by not giving Him the opportunity to guide us to where He wants us to be. We look around for high profile jobs; we may cling on to 'our ministry' and guard our territory with military precision, and often we do it because again we are desperate to be validated and our gifts to be used. Many of us are not arrogant and self seeking, we just want to further the kingdom and make God pleased.

Paul writes in Romans *"For as we have many members in one body, but all the members do not have the same function"*[32]. As I have already touched on there are certain ministries within the church which God has specifically ordained people to fulfil. There are ministers and others, who will display distinct gifting to teach, preach, evangelise and prophecy. However while we are not all prophets, we are all called to be a prophetic people, listening to the Spirit of God and moving with Him. We are not all called to be Evangelists but we are called to carry out the great commission of Mathew 28. We will not all be preaching or teaching in the ministry of the church but we are called to learn of God and to be ready with answers [33]. And we are all, as Paul says in 1 Corinthians 13 [34] called to apply the attributes of love over everything that we do

God wants us to succeed and feel good about ourselves because He loves us, He knows that half the time we are running around like headless chickens doing things which we think He wants us to do. The sad truth is that many times we should be doing none of the things we are. One of the biggest cries from church is that 100% of the work is done by 25% of the people, and maybe that statistic doesn't apply to your church but I can still imagine that it isn't far off. In every church there is a core of people who seem to pick up whatever job needs to be done leaving a majority who are not so involved. When this happens the relationships in that core group are stretched at home, at work and at church because of their impending burnout.

If we took those same people and put them in a situation where they didn't take on any duty unless God had directed them, if we added leadership who didn't start anything unless God was directing them, and if that leadership encouraged others to actively discover what God wanted them to do at that time what a different church we would have. Because **all** of the church would be walking in the Spirit, using their gifting in the way God wanted and **knowing** that if He was telling them to do it, then they had all the resources in them including the time. That equals, no burnout, and the whole church moving as one. We know what happens when the church move forward as one, because it happened in the upper room at the very beginning of the church ; Acts 2 v 1-4.

If He is welcomed and allowed God will envision the leadership of each church and under their guidance the people will be directed and built up in Him. The Holy Spirit never contradicts Himself so when He starts to direct a minister to the things He wants for a church He speaks to all those who are listening in the fellowship.

But what happens when the minister is not listening to God but the people are? Understand that leadership is God's problem and not yours. Pray hard and God will tell you to stay while He changes things where you are, or He will direct you to another fellowship while He deals with any problems with the minister at the previous church. It is not our place to work against those in leadership. However you feel, all leadership has been placed there by God and comes directly under His authority and guidance. No Christian should work against their leadership, and there is no circumstance at all which is beyond God to redeem or restore. All dissention does is to help the enemy with his job and it is a powerful weapon in his armoury. If you have been party to this sin repent and ask God to forgive you and confess it to your minister and also ask their forgiveness. [More on this in spiritual healing].

We are very fortunate to belong to a church which has been given a clear vision from God and is working through that vision at an individual, corporate, and leadership level. God has directed us to this church and will use both myself and my husband in its ministry, we don't know how yet He hasn't fully shown us but we are patiently waiting and as He prompts us we will say "yes".

Many churches will ask "what is your gifting, and where your talents are?" and all of us could say where and in what capacity we have been used in the past. However we need to be careful not to let where we have been limit the area in which God wants to use us now. In Exodus 16 God tells Moses that He would feed Israel with manna each day but they should not gather more than they needed to as it would not keep. Each day they gathered and were filled but some kept it overnight and it was unusable. God wanted Israel to trust that He would feed them miraculously; He wanted them to rely on Him totally for everything, to deny self and to understand His love for them and His provision. He wants no less for us. We should never stay in the past relying on its glories or crippled by its failings because every day God has new 'manna' for us, using us in ways we would never have dreamt of. It's not that the past has no value, of course it has, the sum of you is your experience but we should never let it limit or compartmentalise our use in the Kingdom of God and in our fellowships.

This life Jesus speaks about; that we would do much more than He did is there at our fingertips. He never made an empty promise or spoke an empty statement. We would heal more powerfully, we would quell the storms of nature more dramatically, we would provide for more lavishly, we would live more graciously, we would speak more effectively, we would raise the dead in a more spectacular way, and we would love prolifically. Every gift Jesus had has also been gifted to us, passed down by the Holy Spirit so that we can bring healing and salvation promises to a dying world. Why then would we limit that for the sake of doing it our way? It makes no sense.

When we take hold of all that God has for us we step out of the discord of this world and into His Shalom; the perfect peace of God.

Chapter 6

The Shalom of God

The traditional Hebrew greeting 'Shalom Aleikhem' means 'Peace upon you', and refers to a very special kind of peace, the peace that passes all understanding and which comes directly from the Father- heart of God.

The journey that Israel took from Egypt to Canaan was long and arduous; it involved sacrifice and painful lessons that were learnt along the way. But at the journey's end there was a land full of goodness and rest. Our journey from the world to salvation and beyond is the same. We learn the same lessons, and to trust God along the way. And if we continued on living in His rest then our lives would enter that peace to a greater rather than lesser extent. God's purpose has been the same since the beginning of time, to gather His people, direct their journey and bring them into a place of perfect peace and rest.

"For God so loved the world that He gave His only begotten Son, that whoever believes in Him should not perish but have everlasting life"[35]

Alongside that everlasting life that Jesus brings comes something equally as precious; His Shalom. God's Shalom [Peace] is at the very centre of His rest, when we are in God's rest we are in God's peace; His complete love.

In Luke we read of the angels who came to bring their worship to Messiah at His birth, they cry out *"Glory to God in the highest: and on earth, peace [Shalom], goodwill towards men"*[36]

In Isaiah the prophet pens these words *" Of the increase of His government and peace [Shalom] there will be no end..."*[37]

Strong's concordance says this about this wonderful gift; "Shalom; Completeness, wholeness, peace, health, welfare, safety, soundness, tranquillity, prosperity, fullness, rest, harmony, and the absence of agitation or discord."

So let us look at those listings in Strong's Concordance which give us so much and try to unpack the implications of a life lived in them.

Our Welfare

God's primary concern for us is to bring us into the opportunity of relationship with Him through our salvation bought by Jesus on the cross. After that and for the remainder of our lives He is concerned about our spiritual, physical and emotional wellbeing. Everything He does is done with the express aim to build us up and to take care of us. You see, God loves us. It's an easy statement to make but much harder to understand. Some of us will grasp the theology of it but will miss the truth of it. Some will proclaim it but not live in the benefit of it, and some will just simply disbelieve it, and it's not completely our fault.

God's love is unfathomable; we cannot, in truth, grasp hold of all that it means because of our humanity. But we have to try, because if we don't look closely enough at Him loving us we will never grasp His complete focus on our welfare.

So what is love? People have through the ages tried to quantify the word love, and even on a human scale, to most of us, it is a mystery. Some would quote the feelings and emotions that you get when you think about someone you love. Some would speak of the actions that you would do for someone you love. Some would describe the physiology that happens to the body when they are close to someone that they love.

But surely all of these things are a result of love and not love itself?

A few years ago I was at a ladies conference at Sizewell Hall in Suffolk, the main speaker Jenny Rees-Larcombe had just prayed for me and I was feeling that something was about to happen. I went up to the large room which was used for the main meeting and I sat for a while. After ten minutes or so I felt God tell me to look out of the window so I got up and went to one of the large windows facing the beach. He asked me what I saw, for a moment I was perplexed thinking I should be seeing something out of the ordinary but there was nothing unusual there. "I can see the sea Lord" I replied.

As I stood there I felt God speak these words to me and it changed my life "Imagine that sea is my love, I am going to put one drop inside your heart". In my arrogance I quickly replied "No, Lord, make it two" "Two would break it" He said. I could embellish this story by saying I felt warm fuzzy feelings but the truth is I didn't. Nothing happened immediately, but gently I began to have a clearer understanding and love for those around me, and in ways beyond my understanding, God started to use me to bring love to the loveless and hope to those He put in my path - from parents devoid of any self worth to an elderly man on a park bench that I prayed with as through tear filled eyes he gave his life to Christ.

God loves us! More than that, He cares about us, this Creator, Redeemer, Saviour and Mediator cares. He cares about your relationships, your health, your finance, your sin, your family, your job. Every aspect of your life He wants to be involved in, and He wants to help. But we have to realise that as far as God's love and our welfare goes we can really only comprehend it on an academic level first and foremost, and believe it as truth. Then as we grow in Him we start to recognize the enormity of His love. If you asked me now what I understand, one of the things I would say is that Gods love is spelt c.o.m.m.i.t.m.e.n.t

He is committed to you and to me, to our welfare and our safety, to providing and sustaining us on every level.

And if you want to see that in graphic detail you look no further than the cross.

In Mathews gospel Jesus says in the opening sentence *"Therefore I say to you do not worry about your life"*[38]. As Christians we can either believe Jesus about not needing to worry or not. Personally I believe Him, and I believe that when my Saviour says "Do not worry" I can rest in that. I can trust that and I can unload all that worry onto Him **knowing** that He has my welfare in His hands.

Many of us have the idea that once God gets us He then looks for jobs for us to do, and much like an ant colony and its queen we spend the rest of our lives feeding, caring and working for Him. This is simply not true and it is a lie that the enemy has spread in order to cripple our walk with God, and leave us feeling worthless when we fail as we most certainly will do.

God has however 'good works' for us, Ephesians 2: 8 says

"For it is by grace you have been saved, through faith— and this is not from yourselves, it is the gift of God— **not by works, so that no one can boast.** *For we are God's handiwork, created in Christ Jesus to do good works, which God prepared in advance for us to do".*

All the 'working' in the world will not save us, and will not make God think anything more [or less] of us. The truth is that the 'good works' God has prepared, Jesus demonstrated, He loved, forgave, stood against demons, healed the sick, fed the poor, gave everything, exuded grace, wept, cared for, built up, encouraged, told the truth, and witnessed to God's power.

Once we have entered into that salvation rest God picks us up and lovingly cares for every detail of our lives whatever we do or don't do in the kingdom.

Our Safety

So now we have got a glimpse of understanding that Gods plan involves looking after us on every level let us look at another of 'Shaloms' attributes. I don't know about you but I love scripture. From beginning to end it is full of men and women who have got into trouble in so many ways and yet they have all come through. Some have tried it their way and come unstuck while others have had circumstance hit them between the eyes. It doesn't matter whether trouble is self inflicted or not, God keeps us safe.

In God's rest we can rely on our safety, it is a fact that we are safe in Him. Does that mean that nothing bad happens? Of course not! Life is what it is, but our place in Christ gives us the ultimate security blanket which is not only slung under us, it envelopes us. We can be sure that we are safe...even in death.

I can imagine that Noah looked out at those scoffing friends as he built the ark in the middle of the desert and had a wobble or two even up to the time of the first raindrop. And I can see how the raging torrent that it became, pounding underneath that enormous vessel, would have caused more than a few anxious moments. But Noah was safe in the knowledge of God, and stood, not understanding every detail in God's plan, but resting in the fact that He had one.

As Abraham tied his youngest son to the altar having gathered the wood for the sacrifice, and watched as Isaac looked up into his dad's eyes, and as he held the blade high in the air ready to surrender this precious child, did his heart pound in his chest? I think so but Abraham rested, trusting in God having a plan, he knew whatever happened God was in control. As Joseph, beaten and sold as a slave by the family he loved, languished in prison for so many years at the hand of a lying mistress, did he wonder where his life was going? In all probability at times he did, and yet he patiently waited without understanding, just knowing that God would deliver him, and he was not proved wrong. And Moses, walking out on what would have been a very comfortable existence into a very different life that was, at times challenging and hard, to lead God's people on a journey from slavery to a promised land that he knew he would never enter. And yet he never turned away, even when they moaned and complained. He understood that Gods plan was bigger than any man.

The writer of the book of Hebrews in chapter 11 speaks of these men of God and many more whose gift of faith in God allowed them to see Him work out His plan sometimes with them and sometimes despite them. They all had one thing in common; they knew that God had His best for them and they trusted Him even when it seemed it had all gone wrong.

In God we are safe even when we cause His plans to be delayed, rescheduled or rethought. In Him we are so precious that even when we mess it up, walk away or get it wrong we are still safe in the love that took Him to the cross.

Paul, in Romans 8 wrote these words *"For I am persuaded that neither death nor life, nor angels nor principalities nor powers, nor things present nor things to come, nor height nor depth nor any other created thing, shall be able to separate us from the love of God which is in Christ Jesus our Lord"*[39] and he knew what he was talking about.

To be honest most of us want to see the whole picture with the map laid out before us so that we know the route and if hazards come we have time to plan and to execute it. "Living by faith" is a term often used for those who are relying on God for their finance and provision whilst doing God's work in the field of mission or service. They have no other regular income and are trusting God to supply their needs, however I would challenge us to think wider and understand that in "rest" we are all "living by faith". Living by faith, does not know the route in advance. It is walking down the road without understanding what is around the corner and facing it head on knowing that God has already prepared for it and will get us through it. It is resting in that knowledge and not trying to sort it out ourselves. It knows that we are safe in Him and have no need to worry about anything, but can confidently hand our concerns over to him and then wait for Him to rescue us - as He will do.

Those of us who patiently wait without seeing any movement from God are tempted to take matters into our own hands, and sadly often we do. There is a real truth in "eleventh hour" rescues and God is a stickler for timing. He never does anything until it is the right time but He always does the right thing and it is always with our physical, spiritual and emotional safety in mind.

Harmony ; The absence of agitation or discord

Paul writes in Philippians *"Not that I speak in regard to need for I have learned in whatever state I am to be content"*[40]

The key word in this verse is the word 'learned'. None of this teaching is automatic. Israel on their wilderness journey 'learned' bit by bit to trust God with everything, to do that they had to 'unlearn' a lifestyle based in Egypt and put on one born in the wilderness. The lessons they took on board were passed down to the next generation who eventually had the privilege of entering Canaan.

When we pick up the post in the morning and discover an unexpected bill which will severely hit our depleted finances how do we react? Mild panic? Severe panic? Pray? At differing times I would have done all three, including cry. Where we are in our spiritual life will determine which phase of reaction we bring when faced with challenges that come our way. Paul had learned to be content even though he was on the way to his execution and knew that the path was set. He wasn't agitated or distracted by thoughts of it, he continued to do the work Christ had commissioned him to complete; to be a disciple of Christ, and to give opportunity to others to do the same through his teaching.

Over the years the Pharisees in Jesus day had increased the number of rules for Israel to obey to a near impossible level. Through their inflexible interpretation of the Torah they had created a people in bondage to the law. Jesus came and threw the rulebook out; He makes it clear that His mission was to bring freedom, not chains, to God's people. He condemned the Pharisees for their judgemental attitude to a people who had no hope of continually keeping all of their man made rules.

True harmony for us will only exist if we grasp hold of the fact that a life resting in God's ability allows us to truly not worry about anything that the day brings. However, if we choose to 'go it alone' and sort things out our way, we start to feel the effect of that inner conflict and discord is the result. We begin to feel that conflict in our spirit as thoughts over the problem start to get stronger, our mind tries to analyse the best way to deal with it and we then take action. This is exactly what the enemy wants. Our focus is now set on the problem and any action we take will result in more focus as we wait to see whether what we have done has solved the problem or made it worse. Compare that to picking the envelope up, opening it, reading it, praying and asking God to provide the extra finance to pay it, and then filing it, waiting for God to show you anything you need to do, and resting in the fact that He will. Sometimes it may be a miraculous provision. Other times you will be blessed in other areas so that those funds will be released for the purpose of paying the bill, it may even be that you are offered additional paid work. Either way, your finance, along with everything else is God's problem.

Does that give the excuse for wild living? Of course not. But do you get the point? Every area of our life fits together like a spiritual and physical jigsaw. The choice we have is letting God put it together, which brings harmony, or us joining it up, which brings discord. God longs for our hearts, our minds and our bodies to be at peace why would we choose to work against that?

Tranquillity

The effect of living in God's rest and allowing Him to bring our life into harmony is that we have tranquillity in our hearts.

My daughter and I have one weekend a year which is "ours". We go to a leisure park near our homes and bed down in the quietness of a woodland lodge. Sometimes we go with a group of ladies and other times with just a few friends. One of the highlights is the Sunday morning when we book a spa session with all of the different rooms to go in to be steamed or heated up with scents of Jasmine and other oils. One room is simply quiet. You cannot hear anything from the outside at all. It has a central pool into which drops of water intermittently fall causing ripples to form and be projected on to the ceiling. On the curved stone benches are large soft cushions for people to lay and doze as they wish and the air is warm, it is almost womblike. Are you there with me? Good. You see when Claire and I go it is usually in January when the weather is cold and frosty outside. But in this room it is totally warm and inviting. Some would say this epitomises tranquillity; somewhere quiet and peaceful, relaxed and unhurried. To be fair, when we come out at lunchtime the harshness of the day is very unnerving for a while. Our ears seem to be more sensitive to the noise around us and without fail each time we have said 'Can we go back in'

For me writing these words down catches my heart because that is what God longs for with us; to take us to a place where we can have that tranquillity, where 'outside' the nature of life jangles in our ears, the pace of the day rushes past us at lightning speed, and our physical body is stretched beyond measure, but 'inside', it is a different thing altogether. Our 'inside' person is quiet, relaxed, peaceful and unhurried, they see the day, they are in the same life and the demands are still the same but they don't have to deal with them in the same way: God is in control, this is His "Shalom".

And this is choice! This inner tranquillity is not a longed- for thing that can never happen. Susanna Wesley mother of John and Charles, had eight children who grew up: and also suffered the pain of losing eleven in infancy. Her household was impoverished and she was responsible for most of her children's education alongside her other domestic duties. At one point their house burned down and she had the job of holding things together in her husband's absence and at the same time held house church services for up to two hundred people and wrote several journals. She got up incredibly early and went to bed late, with no modern appliances to help her. Her days were full on and hectic. However at a point in each day she would sit in the kitchen and put her apron over her head and the children would know that their mother was having her quiet time. Her example stood her family in good stead for in the midst of their turbulent lives, at times when they needed that quiet I am sure her example would have come to mind. We need to choose well and understand that inner tranquillity is ours from God.

Peace

In the Greek of the New Testament the word for God's peace is "Eirene". Some of the attributes of Eirene are security, safety, prosperity and harmony. It also denotes the way that leads to peace [Salvation] and the tranquillity of a soul assured of Salvation through Christ, and was used by Jesus in John 14 v 27 to speak of the peace He gives.

The Old Testament writers use the Hebrew word "Shalom" which according to 'Strongs' concordance and the headings we are now looking at has similar meanings. However Hebrew words go beyond the spoken meaning, they include feelings, emotions and intentions. When we look at the word Shalom we are looking at complete peace, one that envelopes every part of us.

Neither word should be confused with the secular meaning of peace. Shalom and Eirene speak of a God given peace not one that can be obtained through exercise, meditation or discipline.

In the secular world religions which promote peace through meditation and deliberation, use our mind as a place where we can induce deep relaxation, and at the extreme an almost hypnotic state. The secular world also uses this as a tool and things like hypnosis to help with issues that you cannot overcome in life are common. Our enemy must be clapping his hands with glee as even some Christians will succumb to this process as well.

In my opinion anything that allows access to our minds while we are in a place of vulnerability such as a hypnotic state should be avoided. We have an enemy whose battleground is often our thoughts and feelings and giving the slightest possibility of manipulation to him is dangerous.

Some would say that they are a naturally calm person and they exhibit a peaceful life to bear that out and I would not argue with that. Some close friends who are not Christians are very peaceful and choose a laid back lifestyle which allows them to live a life unhurried and phased by life events. Comparing them to other friends who are Christians and racing round stressed and worn out saddens me, especially when they make the comparison.

Peace can be feelings based; we can say 'I feel peaceful today' and that can be the case; dependent on the circumstances that we are in.

One of the meanings from the Oxford dictionary is that peace is the freedom from disturbance; tranquillity, mental or emotional calm.

But Shalom peace is a gift, and as such, like faith it is not able to be accessed by those outside the family of God. It is set aside like every other gift to help us become the people that God wants us to be and to strengthen our journey along the way and is ours through the gift of salvation and Jesus' sacrifice on the cross. It is a 'fruit' of us living and moving in the gifts of the Holy Spirit and His leading; it transcends all human understanding and guards our hearts and minds in Christ Jesus [41]. It allows us to be in the midst of the storms of life knowing our anchor is Christ, and this 'Shalom' is our position and not our opinion. It is what is available to us and it is not dependant on our feelings or our circumstances. It speaks more of who we are than what we are demonstrating.

Fullness

In the section on gifts we looked at the fact that when we enter into relationship with God and become Christians we are filled with every gift we will ever need to use.

"Therefore you do not lack any spiritual gift as you eagerly wait for our Lord Jesus"[42].

But that is only part of the fullness that living in God really gives. When we start to operate in God's rest [His completeness] we begin to "decrease", and as we have already said as that happens He will "increase". Bit by bit our lives will become 'His life through us'. We will become filled with Him and He will be able to outwork His plan for us and those in our circle of influence.

Being full of God means living a full life; it is this abundant life that most of us long for. It is the life that Jesus promised in John *"...I have come that they may have life, and that they may have it more abundantly"*[43]

Abundant life means life in large quantity, plentifully, copious, rich, profuse, lavish. God wants your life to be lavish, rich and plentiful, not limited, dour and filled with worry. That's the reason Jesus came, not just to save us but to give us a relationship with God which brings about a life of abundance filled with every good gift and feeling that you could imagine. Whether you are in a hospital bed on your last day on earth, or at the top of a mountain breathing the sweetness of the air around you, this fullness, this abundance is yours. It is yours not because of anything you have done, are doing or will do, It is yours for the reason God has given it to you, because He loves you passionately, whoever you are, whatever you have done.

So what is holding us back from living in God's abundance? What excuse are we making? Would we live abundantly if we had more finance? Would we live abundantly if we had a job, or had less pain? We could all write a list of the reasons why we feel that this abundant, rich and lavish life is for other people but not for us. I hate to burst your bubble but I have to say that this abundant life is yours, by right. It is part of your inheritance and you already have it, you just don't know it.

When I was a young mother of two I had a prayer partner called Helen, she was 84 years old and a shining example of living in God's abundance. She had suffered from cancer for some years and had had both breasts and lymph glands removed. She then had surgery for both knees and both hips. During her times in hospital under the care of two different surgeons and nursing staff, she led both surgeons in prayers of salvation, with one kneeling at her bedside sobbing in his repentance with her patting his head whilst linked up to a drip. That may not happen to you! But Helen taught me that even in the valley of the shadow of death God uses us to bring His light and this abundant life to those in a dark world. She has long since gone to be with her Saviour and I cannot wait to put my arms around her and hug her in heaven because now finally I understand how she could live the way she did.

This fullness, this abundance is yours right now to tap into, what are you waiting for?

Soundness

Something that is sound is solid, whole and unbroken. In Titus it says this *"He must hold firmly to the trustworthy message as it has been taught, so that he can encourage others by sound doctrine and refute those who oppose it"*[44]

Solid stuff makes a good base to build on! Jesus says that His words worked out in our lives are like the man who built his house on a rock able to withstand the storms that came [45]. We must understand that when Jesus says or does something He is not saying it to other people it actually does apply to us. Every word that Jesus spoke is a rock under our feet, they are the foundation of our walk with God and are a sound platform on which we can build our lives.

In the passage above Titus speaks of sound doctrine. We must be careful about what we take on board in our lives so that we are not led astray and I urge you to take the words you are reading and measure them against scripture. None of us is perfect and although this book will have been scrutinised, if it doesn't match up to scripture it is worthless. God's word is solid, whole and complete, together with His works and when we live in the power of it we are living in completeness just as we said at the very beginning.

In 2 Timothy it says *"For God has not given us a spirit of fear, but of power and of love and of a sound mind"*[46]

God gives us the solid unbroken gift of scripture, a spiritual map to test things against. But that is not all. This scripture tells us that He has given us power and love and a sound mind, that sound mind literally means 'safe thinking'; the ability to understand and to make right decisions.

As we start to unpack this teaching we are discovering that God has not only ordained the journey but He has also equipped us for it and given us the ability not only to understand it but decide to live in the fullness of it. Every day that we choose not to do this we are living a life contrary to the one we have been ordained to have, in rebellion of the gifting He has given to help us do it. Instead of a life built on the promises and power of God we are on shifting sand, open to the various winds that come across our path. If we were powerless in this situation it would be acceptable but the previous paragraph teaches that we are not.

In Acts 3 Peter and John were on their way to the temple to pray at about 3.00pm in the afternoon. Beggars frequented the area looking for alms from the temple worshippers, those unable to work through sickness or physical disability were taken or carried there where they would lay all day calling out to the passers-by. This particular man was known to be placed daily at 'The Beautiful Gate' or Solomon's Portico which was the entrance to the temple and he called out to Peter and John as they approached.

Peter looked straight into his eyes and said *"Silver and gold I do not have, but what I do have I give to you: In the name of Jesus Christ of Nazareth, rise up and walk"*. [47] He then took the man's hand and lifted him up, scripture tells us that 'immediately' the man's ankles and feet became strong and he leapt for joy, walking into the temple with them dancing and praising God. Everyone who witnessed it ran together amazed. Peter then deflected the amazement away from John and himself and confronted them with what they had done to Jesus and who He was. He went on to give Jesus the glory for healing this man.

"And His name, through faith in His name, has made this man strong, whom you see and know. Yes, the faith

which comes through Him has given him this perfect **soundness** *in the presence of you all."* [48]

You and I are broken people, we are broken by illness, circumstance, and attack BUT in Jesus we are sound, whole, healed, and restored and we need to understand that, and live it. God has covered every base in order that we live in this abundance but it is always our choice as to whether we do so.

Health

God wants us healthy, not only physically but spiritually and emotionally. We can relax in the fact that any issues we have in any one of these three areas will be dealt with by God as we acknowledge them and give them into His hands. He will guide us into a place of healing aided by our spiritual family, it doesn't matter which issue is pertinent to you, all issues are the same. When we are talking about health it is in God's heart to bring about wholeness in every area of our lives and to that end He works tirelessly to bring about the right conditions for that to happen. Where our health has been broken for whatever reason, we stand in need of healing and restoration, whether here on earth or in heaven.

There are over 70 references to healing in scripture most in the New Testament. Some are references to the need for healing, some about healing, and some describe the healing. All acknowledge that we have a God who heals us physically, spiritually and emotionally.

More than that, He is not just interested in mending us when we are broken but also in keeping us healthy in the first place so that we won't need healing.

The subject of healing is a very emotive issue and I know that some have had concerns and questions with this subject when prayer just didn't seem to cut through the situation and they lost people they loved. So I will try to bring as faithfully as I can what I believe to be God's heart on health and healing in relation to this teaching.

We are as a people made up of the three components mentioned earlier; physical me, spiritual me, and emotional me so let us examine each individually and then pull them together.

Healing Spiritual me

We can all agree that the foremost evidence of our spiritual brokenness is healed when we take hold of the gift of salvation and become Christians. That gaping hole in our spirit man is filled by the Holy Spirit who comes and takes up residence in our lives bringing a wholeness that we were previously unable to obtain. However, our spirit is not safe from harm and we can sometimes find ourselves in desperate need of spiritual healing several years down the line. Sometimes 'church hurts', an awful statement to make but very true, many good folk are hurt more by other Christians than by the world. We almost expect the world to attack us on our beliefs, our integrity, our values and our lifestyles, but we never expect it from within the church and when it happens the damage is profound.

Church operates differently from the world or at least that's what we believe, but sadly, in many cases, it doesn't and we can find ourselves in the middle of gossip, slander, pain, and rivalry. Many leaders can be spiritually demolished not by attack from the demonic but from their congregations and they often crawl away, totally wiped out by assaults on their character and their ministry. No wonder some end up compromising their integrity just for a peaceful life, in some ways I don't blame them.

Young Christians full of enthusiasm for God, in church like excited puppies are often put in their place and those who are moving in the gifts of the Spirit are carefully moulded into what is acceptable. All this and you had better not sit in the wrong seat in case you offend someone! I am painting a pretty dark picture but the truth is that, although the world can hurt us in many ways, only the demonic and other Christians can hurt us spiritually. We can feel physical and emotional pain by things that come at us from unspiritual areas but our spirit life is only damaged by spiritual things. We know that our spiritual life and not just our emotions have been hurt when our spiritual walk is affected and our relationship with God is hampered.

You may not agree with this and want to ask God whether I have got it right but let's look at it slightly deeper.

When we are with other Christians we feel a deep connection, some call it 'Spiritual coupling', we have a deep centred understanding even with strangers, that is born out of the fact that we share the same inheritance and the same indwelling of the Holy Spirit. It is the thread that connects the family of God together much as genes link us as human families whether or not they live near. This spiritual link is one of the focal points of attack from our enemy. He knows if he can somehow get between us and sow seeds of discord and disruption then he can hurt us and those around us. Now we are aware of enemy tactics, we run seminars and teach on them, we write books about them, preach about them and run courses on how to be set free from them. The truth is that despite all these things that we use, people are still getting hurt.

One of the main tools in the enemy's kitbag is expectation, and I have touched on this before. Expectation in its many guises is one of the most powerful pieces of his equipment, and he wields it with great precision both in his attacks on churches and on individuals. Often the effect it has causes other hurtful problems such as low self esteem, gossip, slander, pride and envy.

Question; when we walk into a new church what are our first thoughts? Are they;

- What's the worship like?
- Is it friendly?
- Is the pastor/vicar good at preaching?
- Is there a good youth program?
- Do they include hymns?
- What outreach do they do?
- Are they involved in mission?
- Do they believe and practice the gifts of the Spirit?

Or is it

- Does God want me here?

You see if we approach church as we approach any other activity in our lives we will always be looking to realize a need in us. We could write a similar list for the supermarket we use, the gym we go to, the restaurant we eat at, all because they will fulfil our criteria. After all we have an expectation of what we require from each one. I would not go regularly to a supermarket that did not give me value for money, stock the food I want, or open at the right times, I would simply find one that did.

And that's what happens with church when we use the same view. We find people coming through the doors with an expectation of what they require and when and if the church stops fulfilling that need, they simply go to another one taking their discontentment with them. But that's not all that happens because before they leave they can cause misery through gossip and mumbling discord about the things or people they have a problem with. That in turn causes unsettled churches, whose congregations remain but have to then deal with the fallout, sometimes resulting in deep spiritual hurt. At best this happens in small pockets, at worst it sees churches split from side to side and immeasurable spiritual damage done both to those who leave and those who stay and it cripples their ministries for years, even decades in some cases and then the enemy sits back in satisfaction, job done!

Now let's look at the second answer, the one that said 'Does God want me here'. We combat the effect of expectation by resting in the fact that if you ask Him God will guide you to the right church. Once you have that as an understanding, you can then rest in the fact that if He has got you there it is because you are needed there at some point. It might be straight away or it may be months down the line, but be assured it's not because of what you can get out of it; it's what you can give.

So if we are now in the church that God wants us in what next? Well next there are three things

- Support your minister/ leadership
- Support those around you
- Allow yourself to be supported

God knows you and knows your spiritual and physical needs. Jesus says in Mathew 7 *"..or what man is there among you who if his son asks for bread will give him a stone? Or if he asks for a fish, will he give a serpent? If you then being evil, know how to give good gifts to your children, how much more will your Father who is in heaven give good things to those who ask Him!"*[49]

Do we believe Him? Because if we do then we will know that He would not lead us into a place where we cannot thrive *[expanded it reads; flourish, prosper, succeed, bloom, blossom, increase]*. He would also not lead us into a place where we could not be used in the way He wants us to be used. Now if we take that on board, whether the worship is what you have been used to, or the preaching, or the chairs or any one of the hundred different elements that make up a church, it won't matter because you will be there because God wants you there and expectation will not be a problem.

How do we deal with spiritual hurt when it does happen, and how do we receive spiritual healing? Repent! This is probably not the answer some may want to hear but it is vital. If you are someone who has been in that place where the enemy has used expectation to damage your view of a church and cause discontentment for you and for others who you have spoken to, firstly you need to repent. Repent of expectation, of being used by the enemy, of allowing gossip and hurtful words and thoughts to take root in your life, and for the damage it did for everyone it affected. Secondly ask God to show you where you should be, are you in the right fellowship or is it one that you thought ticked your boxes? And thirdly don't be proud, with expectation comes the thought process that you should not make yourself vulnerable, tell people, and be accountable for the future so that the enemy will not be able to use the same tactics with you again.

If you are someone who has been hurt by that process and although not directly involved it caused you harm in any way then first and foremost you need to go to God with your pain. So many times we feel a need to go to pastoral support or a friend or someone we trust, and it's not wrong to do that at all, but first you need to go to God and here's why. God knows you, and as good as anyone else is they are not Him and they haven't got His insight. Paul says in 1 Corinthians *"For now we see in a mirror, dimly, but then face to face. Now I know in part, but then I shall know just as I also am known."*[50] However good our friends are they don't come close to understanding us and can't. If however your first contact is to God with a prayer that asks for His guidance He will not disappoint you, and you will be brought to the right person for Him to use to bring restoration of your spiritual life and a healing that will be complete.

I am not against pastoral teams, or prayer partners or counselling in its various forms, but I feel that if we use them first and then God we have got the order wrong, and that can eventually bring about a worse situation than you previously found yourself in. God stills our hearts; He doesn't need to hear the ins and outs of the circumstances because He already knows. And the things you do share from your heart will not affect the situation in an adverse way; He is uniquely unbiased in all things, and His main concern right at that moment is you and you alone. He has the ability to bring instant peace and healing, equally He knows that sometimes a tactile hug and affirmation is what we need so He provides the right shoulder to cry on and strangely it may not be the person we think would be best. But He has no chance to do all of this if we rush off thinking we know who to go to and what we need without consulting Him.

Spiritual healing is a deep and profound matter and will always result in us being in a different place from when we started. The Holy Spirit is committed to our growth in Christ and when we are healed spiritually from hurt we gain ground, we become stronger and more resilient. That's why our enemy is bent on keeping us from accessing our healing; he knows that if he can create the right conditions it will see us in a hamster wheel of healing and hurt, never really reaching freedom. And it's why some Christians are always at the front of the queue for the same problem when a call comes at a healing service for prayer ministry. I would be so bold to say that if you are still talking about a spiritual hurt after receiving ministry for it you have a problem and it's not the hurt itself it's your understanding of who God is and His love for you.

If we decide to take our hurt to our friend first instead of God we immediately have an expectation that they will help. Trouble comes when they don't completely eradicate the hurt and we are perplexed; they have prayed for us before and usually their prayers are powerful so we trundle round to the next prayer opportunity, and so it goes on. Going to God first nips this in the bud straight away, He may still direct you to your friend, He will direct his/her prayers which may well be similar to what they would have prayed anyway, but the difference will be the order. The minute we put situations in God's hands and step back, allowing Him to orchestrate the rest, is the moment we give Him opportunity to not only work on everything around the hurt but begin to work in us to bring about the right conditions for full healing.

God will never barge in uninvited, we are the ones who need to allow Him to work and we will only do that if we have confidence in Him. Spiritual hurt needs spiritual healing and the best place to obtain that is in the Father heart of God. We **can** be confident in Gods ability, Paul writes in Ephesians 3 v 20 *"Now to Him who is able to do exceedingly abundantly above all that we ask or think, according to the power that works in us"*. God will bring us into spiritual restoration if we give Him the opportunity.

Healing physical me

Our physical bodies are amazingly put together. The psalmist speaks of it in Psalm 139 and they put it wonderfully, *"I will praise You, for I am fearfully and wonderfully made; marvellous are Your works, and that my soul knows very well. My frame was not hidden from You, when I was made in secret, and skilfully wrought in the lowest parts of the earth. Your eyes saw my substance, being yet unformed. And in Your book they all were written, the days fashioned for me, when as yet there were none of them"*[51]

We are amazing, and when things are working well we can 'praise Him' as the psalmist said. Unfortunately as a result of the rebellion in Eden by Adam and Eve, creation itself was warped by disease and devastation. The perfection which once existed was marred by death and we now live in the aftermath of that. If you add mans greed which makes us want to put ourselves in God's place, we find ourselves living in a world where our fragile planet and its inhabitants face a myriad of problems that can and quite often do affect our physical health.

It is sadly a fact that we do get ill and sometimes that illness is serious. We don't tend to pray fervently if we get a cold, and as parents we are quite relieved when our child contracts a 'childhood illness' like chicken pox because it helps to get it out of the way while they are young and it is more inconvenient than life threatening.

But what about cancer, or heart conditions, kidney failure, liver disease, and the other hundred or more diseases that could rob us of these precious days on earth? How do we deal with these? What about addiction to tobacco, to alcohol, to drugs or even to food all of which have the potential to damage our health substantially?

Jesus' time on earth was spent healing and teaching. In most cases when He did one He was doing the other at the same time so it stands to reason that in order to look at this whole subject of physical healing we need to look at Jesus.

In Mathew 20 v 32 we see Jesus on His way to Jerusalem and the cross. This is His final journey on earth and everything must have been in sharp focus. On the way out of Jericho two men were sitting on the side of the road waiting. In this passage we know nothing more about them except that they were blind and we can presume they were begging, the other gospels reveal one man's name - Bartimaeus. As the crowd passed the men heard that Jesus was amongst them and they cried out to Him *"Have mercy on us. Oh Lord, Son of David"* the passage tells us that Jesus stood still and called to them and He asked a question which is as relevant today for our healing as it was to them that day *" What do you want me to do for you?"*. Let us hold that thought.

We know that in salvation one part of what we receive is authority, and that includes authority over sickness. So we have the authority over sickness affecting our bodies, but we have also discovered that we have gifts in direct proportion to our spiritual lifestyle. Big prayers require big lifestyles in God. Our prayers of authority will be less effective the further our lives are from what God would want us to be.

To live in Shalom means that God is imparting health upon us, even when we are sick. Firstly He encourages us to live that 'big' life resting in Him rather than our own ability and that alone gives us a hefty authority over sickness. Secondly He asks that question *"What do you want me to do for you"* but that is a question He asks the person who is sick, not the people praying for them. The answer to that question is a very personal one and cannot be answered by those around. What we tell Him may be very different from the answer our friends and loved ones might give. They may beg for us to be healed, restored to them and for life to be normal again. We, on the other hand, when faced with a changed life on earth or one which will include more treatment and a substantial loss of ability might say "Lord, I want to be with you. Look after my family". That conversation is between us and God and may never be shared, as we presume that everyone would want to stay here rather than go to His side. From our perspective maybe we would not want our families to think we would want to leave them.

However alongside understanding our spiritual authority over sickness and our need to live a lifestyle that maximizes its potential we need to consider God's grace. Grace [charis] comes from the same Greek root as 'chara' which means joy. It causes rejoicing and signifies unmerited favour or undeserved blessing and it one of Gods gifts; *"But to each one of us grace was given according to the measure of Christ's gift"*.[52] So even when our lives don't measure up to those big prayers, and we falter in our belief that we have authority over the sickness God comes exuding His grace over the situation and brings healing.

God's grace is abundant but it also a mystery that can often puzzle us, for sometimes when we have prayed big prayers, stood in authority and waited for God's grace, healing still doesn't happen. We need to understand that for the most part we have a limited human perspective on life, we tend to see it as the circle around us; our families, our loved ones and those whom God has given us a heart for, it may be the elderly or the young or those on the mission field. But our line of sight is imperfect; we don't see the bigger picture. God does and He also sees our heart cry.

There were occasions where Jesus healed with seemingly no input from the sick person at all, but in fact healed them on the supplication of those around, as He did in the case of the Centurian and his servant. There were also times where Jesus healed spontaneously as He did when He came across the widow whose son had just died, scripture tells us that He had compassion on her and restored the boy's life. That is Grace in action and outside all of our big lifestyle, actions, prayers and supplications; that is simply down to the love of God.

Jesus says in Mathew 7 v 7 *"Ask and it shall be given to you, seek and you shall find , knock and it will be opened to you"* That is a really important verse, If Jesus says that and you couple it with the previous verse you have Him saying to us "Ask me what you want me to do and I will do it" [paraphrased] and the reality is that if God says that then we have to believe that it is true. And if we go down that route as Christians, then the truth is that every person who calls out to Jesus in their sickness is answered in the same way and their wishes are met. Sometimes we will never know that conversation has taken place, and the person involved will go home to be with the Lord because they have told Him that's what they want. At other times, as with my friend Lesley who was diagnosed with cancer three days before she died, we will know because they will tell us what they prayed as she did.

So where do we stand then as Christ's witnesses when someone who we know is sick? What do we pray? The truth is that if we only prayed what God was laying on our hearts to pray instead of praying what we thought we ought to pray it would change our outlook completely. I was in a small prayer meeting as a very young Christian and all those around me were praying for our Pastor's mum who had terminal cancer. They all prayed really good heartfelt prayers of deliverance and healing over her, I sat quietly in the corner my heart pumping as God showed me this picture of a giant elastic band attached to the lady and stretching to heaven and I felt Him say "Their prayers are keeping her from me, tell them to release her into my will". With a very dry mouth I told them the picture as her son sat in front of me and it was one of the hardest things I have ever done. Our Pastor smiled, and without hesitation, said "That feels right" and prayerfully released his mother into God's will. Nothing immediately got worse and she happily continued coming to church, but shortly after that prayer meeting the Lord took her home.

Sometimes our prayers don't achieve what we feel they should not because they are wrong but just because it may be the wrong time. All of these things should help to create in us a passion to stay closer to God so that He can communicate where and what we are to pray.

I was, together with many others, praying for John Wimber as he battled with throat cancer. For months I found myself praying prayers asking God to strengthen him and to stay close to him during his treatment and for him to be healed. One day I found myself in the park praying. I remembered that I hadn't prayed for John that day so I immediately started to focus on him and his situation but this time I found myself crying out to God for his healing. I hadn't got very far into the prayer when God very clearly told me to stop, I thought it was the enemy so I started to pray more fervently but God spoke again and told me to stop. I opened one eye and then the other and asked God why. The answer He gave really took me aback "I am bringing him home". I never prayed for his healing again but God prompted me to pray around his health and his passage home and I did that until some months later God fulfilled what He had spoken to me that day and John left this earth to be with his Saviour.

Whether we are a member of the congregation, or an elder who has been called to pray for the sick, God in His grace uses us to pray the things on His heart for those who struggle with sickness. Sometimes He just wants to take them home, sometimes they want to go. A lot of the time our prayers are there to sustain them, to place a hedge of protection around them and to bring about the things God has for them even in their illness. A prime example of that is the previous story about Helen and her surgeons.

I had the privilege of working professionally as well as worshipping with a family whose youngest daughter in the world's eyes would have been classified as "severely disabled". Truthfully she had many difficulties, with long periods of time in hospital and was close to death on several occasions. Throughout her time on earth she never shared the gospel or in fact did anything more amazing than love those around her, and fight every day to be all that she could be in God. Over the years her family made contact with people that they would never have been able to touch without her. The way that they lived in God spoke more about Him than any sermon I have ever heard. When she died, the church was full and her mother, smiling delivered the most amazing testimony. There were no dry eyes as she spoke about a God who cares, loves, sustains and comforts, and a daughter set free from the body she had here to a new one that could run through the fields of heaven. The little girl's father had been broken some years before by gossip and harsh words as he stood in leadership of the church and he had eventually stood down. God dictated me a letter for him which I delivered. In it He spoke of how the years spent loving his little girl with her broken and dysfunctional body and how he had loved her unconditionally would now be used in pastoring this little broken church. Months passed but eventually he took his place as senior pastor of that church, a changed man, with a father's heart for Gods people trained by a seven year old girl.

God, you see, looks at the big picture, the one that has a beginning and an end and He is determined to see it fulfilled. If you could see the big picture of your life, where it's been where it is now and where it is going, you would see people as yet unmet, situations not yet unfolded and opportunities that you could barely dream of. Resting in the fact that Father God knows us and all our days may help us combat fear, anxiety and concern over them, even when it includes sickness.

We have already touched on the fact that there is an order in God dealing with things and that sometimes He has to cut away at the roots of a situation before He gets to the actual problem itself. Some of us struggle, not necessarily with illness but with potential causes of illness, even some Christians are subject to more alcohol than is good for them, some smoke and there is a large number of us who are overweight.

Our health in God must cause us at some point to look at these aspects of our lifestyles and the potential impact on that 'health' that God gives us in His 'shalom' peace. There is though a certain pressure on each of us to work on these issues ourselves but that is like cutting off the plant above the surface, sooner or later it grows again. God knows the reason that you have the extra glass of wine. He knows why biscuits dull the pain, and He knows why tobacco helps you cope. Quite often we don't! It's always the expectation of both ourselves and others around us that cause us to do the inevitable examination of our lives followed by a self help program that may work for a while until our resolve or pressure causes us to fold and reach for the biscuit or glass of alcohol to make it better.

God will honour your prayer if you go to Him and ask for help in this area but it may not be immediate. He will take you into His timing however frustrating that is and deal with the causes of the issues before the issue itself is even looked at. I have been dieting for years in fact I was a serial dieter. My weight has been as low as

9stone and as heavy as 17stone 9lb. Like many others I realised that this was not healthy and longed to be thin, trying every diet in the book. In 2009 I began to be taught by God about living in His rest and by the end of the year I was excited by the possibilities that it opened. However it wasn't until 2010 that I really started to live the teaching and let go of control in many areas, letting God have them instead. God began dealing with issues some of which had been buried for years, and I started to feel the freedom happening. Earlier this year He addressed my weight, and now I have lost more in recent months than I had done in the past 20 years. You see His timing and His ways are perfect *"As for God His way is perfect; The word of the Lord is proven; He is a shield to all who trust in Him"* [53].

When we allow God to take our pain, our sadness, our sin and our worry, and then trust Him to work it out, without taking it back, we enter into that peace which only comes from Him. And the healing of our bodies, whether here on earth or in heaven which is ultimately where we all receive healing, can really take place.

Healing emotional me

We have already looked at how we can only be hurt spiritually by the spiritual, but our emotional hurts can come from anywhere. These are the things that cause resentment, anger, upset and offence to our feelings. They are not spiritual issues, but they may feel as if they are, especially if they come as a result of upset through our Christian contacts.

Feelings are transient and dependent on a huge number of variables. Our reactions to things will be different when we are stressed from when we are relaxed, tired or wide awake. We all learn not to talk about critical family issues when the children are screaming and tea is bubbling away on the stove, if we do we will get a different reaction from our partner than if we waited until the children were in bed and the house was quiet.

But what happens when we do get hurt, when our feelings are trodden on and we feel disrespected by those around us? How should we deal with that, and how do we receive emotional healing? Well again we can deal with it ourselves or we can deal with it with God. The outcome of hurtful situations will be dependent on that primary decision.

Initially if we go to God He will point to the biblical principle that we should always apply which is outside our emotions. Jesus says in Luke these words *"Take heed to yourselves. If your brother sins against you, rebuke him and if he repents forgive him. And if he sins against you seven times in a day, returns to you saying I repent, you shall forgive him"*[54] There is the little word "if" in there and Jesus does not elaborate on that but in Mathew Peter asks Jesus this *" Lord how often shall my brother sin against me and I forgive him? Up to seven times?" Jesus said to him "I do not say to you up to seven times, but up to seventy times seven"*.55 So I think it's probably a good thing that we adopt an attitude of forgiveness whatever the circumstances.

Forgiveness is not a feeling; it is an act of our will. We don't have to have a warm fuzzy attitude to someone who has just hurt us badly, but we do have to forgive them. Without forgiveness there is no restoration for them or for us. I am not glossing over how hard this is, and sometimes how impossible it feels. I personally know that feeling.

Some years ago someone who I considered very godly and was my mentor hurt our family in the extreme, they did things that I could not contemplate anyone, let alone a person of God doing. I was pregnant with our youngest child and we went through our own private hell. They escaped prison, and I blamed myself because I had prayed that God would punish them in the way He wanted to, I just didn't bank on Him not agreeing with how I thought they should be punished and for some time I was angry with Him as well. Years later, God very gently brought me to a place where, sobbing, I forgave them. To this day I have never had the opportunity to say the words to their face, but I know I will because God has been asked by me to help make that happen.

He is the God of the impossible. Your sin, my sin, through every generation back to Adam caused God to watch His Son go through an agonising death in order to restore us. There is nothing that happens to us in life that comes close to that pain. So He knows where you are, whatever has happened to you.

On the cross Jesus called out *"Father forgive them for they know not what they do"*[56]. It is a cry that spans the centuries because right now, in heaven, every day, Jesus stands as our intercessor before the mercy seat of Father God and cries the same prayer over your sin and mine. So firstly we forgive as an act of our will. We decide and then we say the words, irrespective of the outcome. Don't wait for fuzzy feelings!

Secondly we need to rest in the fact that once we have put it into Gods hands He will show us what to do next, it may be nothing. Our act of forgiveness is a catalyst for God to work in and with the person that we have just forgiven as well as us. An unforgiving attitude wraps chains around you both, so it is vital that we understand how important that first step is. God may seem to have forgotten and the person carries on as normal, but that's a lie that the enemy would sow in order to breed resentment. The truth is that God loves you but He also loves them and that love is a guarantee that He is working to bring restoration to you both.

Emotions are tricky things because quite often we think that if we feel it then it must be true. This is especially real when it comes to us being offended. Offence is a big issue and because of that fact alone we can be fairly certain that it is in the enemy's arsenal.

Worse still than being offended is taking offense on someone else's behalf. How often has someone confided their hurt to a friend who up until that moment may have had a good relationship with the person who is at the centre of the talk but afterwards rebuffs that person as if they themselves have been the one offended. And so it goes on working through whole groups of friends or sometimes whole churches. In 'The Message' Pauls letter to the Galatian church puts it so well *"You were running superbly! Who cut in on you, deflecting you from the true course of obedience? This detour doesn't come from the One who called you into the race in the first place. And please don't toss this off as insignificant. It only takes a minute amount of yeast, you know to permeate an entire loaf of bread. Deep down, the Master has given me confidence that you will not defect. But the one who is upsetting you, whoever he is will bear the divine judgement"*[57]

Don't listen to friend's hurts with ears that cannot be impartial. As it says in the passage, that is God's business and He will deal with things as and when we let Him and when He does, it is done properly.

So, emotional hurt is best dealt with by God on the heels of us forgiving those who have caused the pain. We can then rest in the fact that God knows what He is doing and that all will be well. But sometimes, even when things are seemingly resolved, we are still left with a nasty taste in our mouth over the issues and we have an enemy who keeps reminding us of how bad the pain was. So how do we deal with that?

Quite often feelings will continue on far past the resolution and when they come, as we have just said, they will [with help] jog our memory of how badly we were hurt. It is at this point that we have to dig in and understand the difference between feelings and truth. We know that if we have given the situation to God, He is working it out; that is truth and despite what we feel we need to stand in that truth. If necessary going again and again to God and saying "Lord I know this is dealt with, please help me give to you these new reminders of the hurt and bless [*name the person*] as you do this" The enemy is not going to give up trying to destroy your walk with God. He is determined to use whatever he can to take advantage of us hurting each other, and the mind scars just as easily as the body, sometimes more deeply. In the book of Romans Paul says this *"Do not conform to the pattern of this world, but be transformed by the renewing of your mind. Then you will be able to test and approve what God's will is—his good, pleasing and perfect will* [58]. Paul is talking about our whole selves being given to God's service here but it is equally true in the context that we are looking at. The world's pattern says 'React', look for retribution and hang onto the pain, but Gods way is to forgive, forgive, forgive and leave the situation with Him.

Our mind is the centre of our emotions, our reasoning, and our intellect and it often where we are attacked the most. Very few of us are physically hurt by others but there are many whose lives have been emotionally wrecked by those around them, and still live in that pain. If that is where you are today it is not too late. Take a moment, go to God in a quiet place and tell Him, forgive those involved, lay it at His feet step back and walk away. Then, understand it is now His business. If you have to, keep laying it at His feet until one day your feelings align with the truth; that it is finished and you are free.

God is only interested in our wholeness, our completeness in Him and He will do and say whatever it takes to get us there, listening and standing on His truth is the platform to being healed.

Perfectness

It is quite fitting to follow the previous section with this one. In Colossians 3 the title reads 'Character of the New Man' and it says this; *"Therefore as the elect of God, holy and beloved, put on tender mercies, kindness, humility, meekness and longsuffering bearing with one another and forgiving one another, if anyone has a complaint against one another, even as Christ forgave you so you also must do. But above all these things put on love which is the bond of perfection. And let the peace of God rule in your hearts to which also you were called in one body; and be thankful."* [59]

This passage is quoted from the New King James version. In the NIV 'perfection' is translated 'perfect unity'. Whichever we use, the truth is that 'in Christ' we are made perfect and can live in that perfection. You don't feel perfect do you? Neither do I, but as we have said before truth has nothing to do with feelings.

When Jesus took our sin on the cross, God turned away. It wasn't because He did not love Him and it wasn't that He wanted to 'forsake' Him, it was simply the fact that God cannot be party to sin, the two are like oil and water. When Jesus absorbed our sin, He effectively allowed the sin to separate Himself from God for the first time in history. That one act bought back mankind. The sinless man, pure, whole and perfect, God incarnate became the way for you and me to have a personal relationship with our creator.

When we accept salvation God sees us and our lives filtered through Jesus and it is for that reason we are made perfect 'in Christ'. 'Perfect,' in the context of the text talks about love giving us 'perfect unity' with God, with ourselves and with others. When we allow God to love us and we love others we become united with God and that unity is a very powerful word.

In Acts 1 v 12-14 we read of a prayer meeting going on in the upper room, Jesus had just ascended back to heaven and the disciples had returned from the event and gathered where they were staying. The passage tells us who was there; Peter, James John and Andrew;

Philip and Thomas; Bartholomew and Mathew; James the son of Alpheus and Simon the Zealot, and Judas the son of James. The women were also present together with Mary Jesus' mother together with His brothers. In v 14 it says this *"These all continued with one accord in prayer and supplication...."*

This prayer meeting was undoubtedly very poignant. It was the first time that this group of people had met without Jesus, but meet they did and the text tells us that they were of 'one accord' it translates *homothumadon* and means being unanimous, having group unity, or having one mind and purpose.

It is vital if we want to be in that place where we as church are moving forward, that we are of 'one accord'. Jesus spent three years facilitating a love between these rough and ready men and women and when that love was brought to fruition we see that perfect unity that provided the pathway for what happened next.

In the following chapter of Acts [Acts 2 v 1-4] we see not a handful of men and women but a hundred and twenty gathered together in Jesus' name, a solid block of believers who loved and accepted each other and who were hungry with expectation. All the others had gone back to their previous lives; some disillusioned, some impatient, some who couldn't be bothered anymore. What was left were a people united not only in love but in intention and God did not disappoint, the Holy Spirit descended and the rest is history.

So, if we are made perfect by love as individuals, imagine what God can do through us when we have one mind and purpose!

Again as you can probably guess unity is really high on the enemy's hit list. Disrupting it and causing problems between individuals, as we have already seen, has a knock-on effect on the power of the church you are in. The effectiveness of your church's ministry will be severely capped if disunity is allowed to be perpetuated. Now no Christian would ever say that their assignment in life is to stop the church fulfilling its mission. Indeed most would throw their hands up in horror at the implication. However, by not truly taking hold of the promises of God, living in the power of them, resting in the truth of them and allowing feelings to overpower that truth, we could find ourselves being of considerable value to the enemy's cause and our church could end up limping along instead of marching in power. The truth is that in God's Shalom peace that perfect unity is our position, it's what is given to us, we have it! We are united in God's love by the Holy Spirit, at one with Christ, and made perfect by His love. So let us take hold of that unity with each other and determine to let nothing destroy it!

Prosperity

If you are like me the first thing I think about when I hear the word prosperity is wealth and worldly abundance. Indeed if someone is described as prosperous in earthly terms we know that they are quite well-heeled and live a lifestyle that accompanies that wealth.

There are some Christian ministers who tell us that we should be prosperous and that indeed tithing into Gods kingdom will bring about a time of prosperity for us. In some circles this is known as 'the prosperity gospel'.

If we look up the word prosperity in the dictionary and examine its synonyms it says 'wealth, affluence, opulence, riches, success'. But if we look at the biblical meaning we see something very different.

The Hebrew word for prosper is Chashar pronounced *Kahshar* and it means: To be right, successful, proper, and correctly aligned with certain requirements and it is the word that eventually in post biblical times gives rise to the word *'kosher'*.

It occurs three times in the Old Testament; the first passage uses the word success instead of prosper in Ecclesiastes *"If the axe is dull and one does not sharpen the edge then he must use more strength; But wisdom brings* **success***."*[60]. In other words the wise man accomplishes what he sets out to do and gets the job done more efficiently than the foolish man who the writer compares to a dull axe. The second reference is in Esther 8 "....and says *'If it pleases the king, and if I have found favour in his sight and the thing* **seems right** *to the king and I am pleasing in his eyes, let it be written to revoke the letters devised by Haman, the son of*

Hammedatha the Agagite, which he wrote to annihilate the Jews who are in the king's provinces"[61]. Here Esther pleads for her people to the king, and yet submits herself to his will stating that it would be his discretion that would define whether it **'seemed right'** to him to do what she was asking him to do. The third reference is again in Ecclesiastes 11 *"In the morning sow your seed, and in the evening do not withhold your hand; For you do not know which will **prosper**, either this or that, or whether both alike will be good"*[62]

So in God's terms the word 'prosper' is not about wealth, it is about success in what we set out to do. It is about aligning ourselves with what is right and good and proper, it is about accomplishment and triumph over adverse conditions and it is about living a victorious life.

When we live in God's rest we are aligning ourselves with Him in every aspect of our lives, we are successful in what we do because we only do what He is telling us to with the gifts He has already given to accomplish it. And in that we will prosper in a way that may indeed cause us to be stewards of money and influence so that He can use us in the corridors of power. Equally we can be slaves like Esther, plucked out by the hand of God to bring Him glory in her humility.

Wherever we are in life we cannot buy Gods favour, certainly not by tithing. Tithing is a freewill offering given by us out of the abundance that God has already given to us. The ministries that proclaim that "if we give we get" from God in my opinion are wrong. Biblically scripture calls us to give our tithe however God blesses us with His abundance whatever our giving.

God calls us to give out of our hearts; the tithe was and is always a 10% of produce and /or income. He calls us to be 'cheerful givers' and Jesus gives the example of the widows mite in the gospel of Mark *'Now Jesus sat opposite the treasury and saw how the people put money into the treasury. And many who were rich put in much. Then one poor widow came and threw in two mites, which makes a quadrans. So He called His disciples to Himself and said to them " Assuredly, I say to you that this poor widow has put in more than all those who have given to the treasury; for they all put in out of their abundance, but she out of her poverty put in all that she had, her whole livelihood".'*[63]

In the book of Malachi it says *"Bring the whole tithe into the storehouse, that there may be food in my house. Test me in this,"* says the Lord Almighty, *"and see if I will not throw open the floodgates of heaven and pour out so much blessing that there will not be room enough to store it."*[64] And that tells us that God gives us blessing out of our obedience to Him. The widow who passed by her Lord and Saviour that day in order to give what she did to 'Gods temple' was living out Malachi 3 just as much as those who gave more, and in fact Jesus states in His [God's] eyes she gave more than they ever could. I have a healthy respect for biblical truth, and I don't find it in something that contradicts scripture. I may be wrong and if I am, I pray that God shows me but I can't find a place that speaks of being prosperous as a reward for giving money into certain ministries and receiving blessing as a result. I do however see evidence of Him honouring our giving/tithing and I see evidence of people giving out of their hearts.

All this helps us to see again that prosperity is an attribute of our living in God's rest and accessing His Shalom peace. It is something we have, not something we need to attain. It is not monetary wealth but an abundance of His blessing.

Jesus is the ultimate example of living a prosperous life even unto death. Every day He aligned Himself with Father God and lived in that 'right place'. Even Satan could not tempt Him to sin and compromise His mission to save us. He had no house or worldly goods to call His own; the one garment He wore was a seamless cloth which was taken from Him on the cross. And yet He lived in Gods prosperity, He had more in Godly wealth than Solomon; He was in total alignment with God and accomplished all that was asked of Him. And on His last day here on earth He completed the definitive victory against all things unholy.

We can live in that same place in God! It is not beyond us because God is bigger than everything that would set you up to fail. The only limitation in our lives is our perspective and our disbelief that the same God who empowered Jesus empowers us.

Completeness.

I started writing this book out of obedience to what I believe God is calling His church to be. Over the years we have heard many people cry 'Revival' in this world with pockets of the manifestation of God's power being seen, however they shine like matches that are lit and burn for a while before gradually dying out. That link that God gave to me between His completing creation and His Son completing salvation is the key to all that has been written.

God longs for us to live in the completeness of Jesus' mission, knowing that when God made us; starting with Adam, He made us complete. Our brokenness for countless generations was a source of utmost pain for God. He has watched as people flapped around trying hard to mend themselves. Jesus is the answer to that brokenness and only He is able to make us whole.

When Jesus came He came to make us complete, to change us into a people of power, with faith that moves mountains, people who stay close to the Father and who complete the individual mission that God has for them, in the safety of being together in 'church'. The church God desires to have moves with His fire, waits on Him and only does what it is told to do.

And you and me are part of that wonderful thing, we are 'church' together but until we learn to live as Jesus did, in God's rest [all that He has done].We will never fulfil all that He longs for us to be. But if we do, if we take hold of this most wonderful thing we will be complete, we will live completed lives not once will there be 'what if' and that statement that Jesus made right at the beginning of this teaching won't be a dream it will be a fact.

John 14 v 12; "Most assuredly, I say to you, he who believes in me, the works that I do he will do also: and greater works than these he will do because I go to my Father".

Write it on a card and stick it in a frame, put a magnet on the back and stick it to your fridge, make a bookmark and put it in your bible. Meditate on it until you believe it and understand this is not a loose sentence it is;

Your inheritance

Your position

Who you were destined to be

Put your name on the dots and live it until you see it.

"Most assuredly, I say to you....................... if you believe in me, the works that I do you will do also: and greater works than these you will do because I go to my Father".

All the way through this book a golden thread has run. Why is it so important to live in God's rest? Well it would take and will take you longer than it's taken you to read this book to understand the full implications of the teaching on its pages. But my hope and prayer is that we can start to understand a little of the life it allows us to live, if we live in what God has done instead of working so hard to do it ourselves.

God's rest allows us to be that complete person. We can stop trying so hard to live up to our own and others' expectations. We become reliant on a God who can, and not a man who can't. We know we have everything, the banquet, not the crumbs. We are equipped, taught, provided for; our life is lived in the power of Christ. We are attentive to hearing His voice, and directed by His hand. We pray for things on His heart and watch for the results. We are built up and not knocked down. We will never be failures, always conquerors. We will not jostle for souls to notch up, but understand that they are on their journey with God as we are. And we will not put the expectations that were heaped on us, onto others. We will be kind, compassionate, long-suffering agents of grace. We will build up our leaders and be quick to repent and to forgive. And we will love, because first He loved us.

Jesus said "It is completed" In Him **we can be**.

Biblical References

All references are taken from the NKJV unless stated

1.	John 10 v 1-5	p2
2.	Gen 2 v 1-2	p7
3.	John 19 v 3	p8
4.	James 2 v 26	p15
5.	1 Peter 3 v 1-2	p24
6.	John 15 v 5	p33
7.	Math 17 v 14-21	p34
8.	Rev 13 v 7	p36
9.	Luke 9 v 1	p39
10.	Luke 10 v 19	p39
11.	John 16 v 13-15	p39
12.	Rev 21 v 1-4	p40
13.	1 Pet 1 v 3-9	p41
14.	Eph 1 v 11-14	p41
15.	Heb 11 v 1	p46
16.	Math 17 v 20	p47
17.	Acts 8 v 9-11	p48

18.	Acts 8 v 15-21	p49
19.	Heb 1 v 6	p50
20.	Heb 11 v 6b	p51
21.	Gal 5 v 16	p55
22.	Rom 7 v 15	p56
23.	Luke 22 v 42-43	p56
24.	Math 26 v 38	p56
25.	Luke 22 v 42	p56
26.	Col 1 v 29	p57
27.	John 3 v 30	p58
28.	1 Tim 4 v 15-16	p59
29.	John 8 v 36	p62
30.	1 Cor 1 v 7	p62
31.	Rom 12 v 3-8	p64
32.	Rom 12 v 4	p66
33.	2 Cor 5 v 12	p67
34.	1 Cor 13 v 13	p67
35.	John 3 v 16	p71
36.	Luke 2 v 14-17	p72

37.	Isaiah 9 v 7	p72
38.	Math 6 v 25-34	p75
39.	Rom 8 v 38	p78
40.	Phil 4 v 38	p79
41.	Phil 4 v 7	p86
42.	1 Cor 1 v 7	p86
43.	John 10 v 10	p86
44.	Titus 1 v 9	p88
45.	Math 7 v 24	p88
46.	2 Tim 1 v 7	p89
47.	Acts 3 v 6	p90
48.	Acts 3 v 16	p91
49.	Math 7 v 9-12	p97
50.	1 Cor 13 v 12	p98
51.	Ps 139 v 14-16	p101
52.	Eph 4 v 17	p104
53.	Ps 18 v 30	p110
54.	Luke 17 v 34	p111
55.	Math 18 v 21-22	p112

56.	Luke 23 v 34	p113
57.	Gal 5 v 7-10	p114
58.	Rom 12 v 2	p115
59.	Col 3 v 12-15	p116
60.	Ecc 10 v 10	p120
61.	Esther 8 v 5	p121
62.	Ecc 11 v 6	p121
63.	Mark 12 v 41-44	p122
64.	Mal 3 v 10	p122